Winning With Purebred Dogs

Success By Design

by Dr. Alvin Grossman and Beverly Grossman
Photoartist, Carl Lindemaier

Doral Publishing

Wilsonville, Oregon
1991

Published by Doral Publishing, P.O. Box 596, Wilsonville, OR 97070. Printed in the United States of America.

Copyedited by Luana Luther
Book Design by Tim Bakke
Sketches by Joe Murray
Typesetting by Pioneer Graphics, Wilsonville, OR 97070

Library of Congress Card Number: 91-70230   ISBN: 0-944875-17-3

Grossman, Alvin.
  Winning with pure bred dogs: success by design / Alvin Grossman, Beverly Grossman.

  p. ; cm.

  ISBN 0-944875-17-3

  1. Dogs–Showing. 2. Dogs–Training. 3. Dog sports. 4. Dogs–Breeding. I. Grossman, Beverly. II. Title.

SF425.G   636.7'088'8   20
                                          91-70230

INTRODUCTION

Most competitive sports have fixed rules and many books to tell you how to succeed. However, the "Sport of Breeding and Showing Purebred Dogs" has but fragmented articles and guidelines to assist the neophyte. Books about the various breeds put you in the know about that breed and offer tips on the best bloodlines, but nowhere is there a concentrated body of information that can take you from a budding neophyte to a successful breeder/exhibitor – at least not until this book came along.

There have been no published rules or guidelines that tell you how you might succeed, indeed survive, in this very competitive sport. Since the judging of dogs is as much an art as a science, there are bruised egos, accusations of politics, cries of "foul" and all the other accouterments of a sophisticated sport. At times, campaigning a champion most closely resembles a free-for-all political campaign.

This book is written from many years of experience. I'm speaking as a graduate of the The College of Hard Knocks when I talk about the best ways to build a strong foundation in your breed, to buy your first really good dog, to get your dog ready to be a winner, and how to avoid disappointment.

Using this book as your step-by-step bible can enable you to succeed and rise to the top in your chosen breed.

FOREWORD

The first thing winners start with is FOCUS. You need to define what success is for you – then focus on it.

Some thoughts on what others have written or said about winning:

Alice P. Cornyn-Selby, in her delightful book *Why Do Winners Win?*, wrote: "Although successful people don't always succeed, they never fail. If they lose today, it's only today's contest. They see life as a series of challenges, and they expect to win. What others call defeat is for the successful a temporary setback, which they intend to correct."

Henry Ford said. "Failure is the inability to begin again more intelligently." This book is for those of you who have been in the dog game for awhile without having much success; it is a chance to begin again intelligently.

Col. David Evans was quoted in the *Chicago Tribune* as saying: "Winners focus on a win the same way a laser focuses on metal and cuts it. Call it unconventional thinking, if you want to...winners will often think in unconventional ways, not just to be unconventional but because they are focusing so intently on a solution."

Alice Cornyn-Selby zeroes in on focusing by pointing out that "winners stop doing what doesn't work." This sounds too simple, too obvious. But take a look at how you are breeding, who is trimming and showing your dogs, what kind of judges you show your dogs to. If it ain't working...STOP. Denis Healy, the former British Exchequer, has a first rule of holes: "If you're in one stop digging."

Lastly, let me give you Selby's list of what winners have:

- Focus
- Curiosity
- Impatience
- A name you're proud of
- Ignorance - a need and a desire to learn
- Chutzpah (nerve)

Winning With Purebred Dogs will use all of these to allow you to have *Success by Design*.

ABOUT THE AUTHORS

Dr. Alvin Grossman holds the position of President/Publisher for Doral Publishing, Inc., a publisher of dog books.

His writings have won for him five awards from the Dog Writer's Association of America, including best article for his "It's All in the Mind" piece and a nomination for best general dog book of the year for his *Great American Dog Show Game*.

Al and his late wife were noted Cocker breeders under the Hi-Boots prefix. They bred 25 champions in only 24 litters over a 25-year period. Their Ch. Hi-Boots Such Brass was a top 10 Sporting Group winner for two consecutive years. He currently judges 19 breeds within the Sporting Group.

He has judged in eight foreign countries, which included the World Show in Amsterdam and the Paris International.

He has authored the following dog books:

> *Breeding Better Cocker Spaniels*
> *The American Cocker Spaniel*
> *The Standard Book of Dog Breeding*
> *The Great American Dog Show Game*
> *The Standard Book of Dog Breeding: A New Look*

His articles have appeared in the AKC *Gazette, Kennel Review* and 24 breed publications on a regular basis.

Beverly Black Grossman worked as an editor for Doral Publishing for several years, and *Winning with Purebred Dogs* represents her first effort at writing a book. In addition to her work for Doral, Beverly's writing has covered a variety of subjects and styles, ranging from poetry to technical manuals. She lives in Oregon with her husband, two children and Frosty, a buff-colored American Cocker Spaniel puppy.

Carl Lindemaier has been photographing a wide range of animals, both pets and wild animals, for 20 years and has won numerous awards for his work with the Professional Photographers of America. A native of Frankfurt, Germany, Carl spent 20 years in business management before returning to school to study fine arts. He lives in Portland, Oregon with his family and enjoys mountain climbing, underwater exploring and tennis.

Beverly Black Grossman

Carl Lindemaier

CONTENTS

PART I - GETTING STARTED

PART II - EXHIBITING

PART III - BREEDING

PART IV - RAISING THE LITTER

PART V

PART I
GETTING STARTED

A show-prospect Shar-Pei

Purchasing Your First Show-Quality Puppy

"getting the lay of the land"

Many beginners attracted to the purchase of a purebred dog often go about obtaining one without a thought of obtaining a show prospect. Truth be known, few people have any idea what dog shows are all about.

It's important to your future in dogs to learn about your chosen breed and how it fits into the American Kennel Club (AKC) scheme of things. Is your breed one that was developed to herd cattle or sheep, guard the home, or hunt with his master? The intent of the developers of a breed gives us clues as to what kind of a personality our dog will have and how trainable he will be as a show dog, obedience dog or a hunting companion.

Attending a meeting of your local all-breed kennel or specialty (dogs of your breed only) club will allow you to talk dogs with your fellow breeders and exhibitors.

Those interested in getting involved in the dog show world need to examine their talents and expectations before entering the arena. While some enjoy the art of breeding dogs, others prefer exhibiting only.

If you enjoy competition, and if you can handle the joy of winning as well as the heartbreak of losing, then you are likely to enjoy exhibiting.

Perhaps you are considering becoming a breeder. The probability of success as a breeder can almost be predicted because successful breeders have specific talents in common: they are creative and artistic; they have an innate sense of balance; they understand spatial relationships; and, they can clearly visualize their ideal dog. Not everyone is cut out to be a breeder, but just about everybody can enjoy some aspect of the dog game. AG

Is it better to buy a male or a female puppy?

Most dog books advise the budding novice to obtain the best bitch ("bitch" is the term for a female dog) he can afford and then to proceed with a sound breeding program. Although this appears to be excellent advice, actually it is not.

Assuming that a novice could recognize an outstanding bitch, what breeder would then sell that bitch to a novice? Even if the novice has the best of intentions and a lot of cash, the breeder of the bitch is unlikely to give up such a treasure. An outstanding bitch is worth her weight in gold to the breeder.

One superior bitch is all it takes to launch an entire bloodline. She is endowed with superior physical features, outstanding personality, mental and physical stability, and the ability to reproduce these traits. Most breeders will not consider selling a bitch of this quality to a novice, for they need to feel certain that the bitch will be shown and bred correctly.

The bitch that is available to the novice is usually of lesser quality. How much less? That depends on the breeder from whom she is purchased, the purchase price, and how much the novice has to offer in return. Ideally, this bitch should be able to produce offspring of better quality than the bitch herself.

As a novice, it is easier to purchase a high quality male puppy than a high quality female puppy. Typically, breeders won't keep a male unless it is vital to their breeding program or is of "Specials" quality. (See Chapter 8 for more information about "Specials" dogs.) Many good male puppies are available, puppies that are capable of having good show careers. However, many of these males end up not being shown due to lack of takers. Usually, breeders are delighted to sell their above-average males to people who are interested in showing.

If you would enjoy exhibiting more than

breeding, or if you would like to begin as an exhibitor and move into breeding later, strongly consider purchasing a male puppy first.

You may be able to lease a bitch. Although bitches offered for lease are usually older, under certain circumstances younger bitches are offered for lease. Typically, the younger bitch will have earned a championship or points toward a championship, or will have already produced a litter. Bitches are offered for lease so that the lessor (the breeder offering the bitch for lease) may make room for younger stock but still control the bitch's destiny.

What about leasing a female?

A typical lease agreement provides that the lessor selects the stud dog and receives part of the litter. The bitch then becomes the property of the lessee (the breeder to whom the bitch has been leased). The lessee usually pays all costs of breeding the bitch and raising the litter.

A lease agreement can provide the novice breeder with a higher quality bitch, the type of bitch who is not usually available to a novice. On the other hand, the novice breeder could get trapped in a bad lease with an undesirable bitch.

There are many different types of lease agreements. Be cautious; put the terms in writing for the protection of all involved. Too often, both sides end up with hard feelings if the lease contract is verbal. You, the novice breeder, may wind up on the short end of the stick if you are not careful. Have at least two other successful breeders review the terms and advise you before you sign on the dotted line.

The best time to select and buy a show-quality puppy is when he is about eight months old. By then the puppy should look close to the way he will look at maturity, he will have gone through most of the awkward stages, he will still be young enough to adjust to a new home, and you may still enjoy him as a puppy.

How old a puppy should I purchase?

A puppy younger than eight months may cost less, but you will be taking a risk. Sometimes a serious fault appears, a fault that is undetectable before the puppy is eight months old. For example, the puppy's second set of teeth may come in bad. If this happens, you will be encumbered with a dog on which you have wasted time, effort, money, and emotion. Your enthusiasm may wane and your breeding program may be set back.

It is better to wait until a puppy is eight months old, to pay more for him, and to risk less.

How in the world do I pick a good puppy?

Before purchasing a puppy, become familiar with the breed. Go to dog shows, talk with breeders and exhibitors, read the breed standards, and read a book about your breed. Recognize, understand, and appreciate the characteristics of your breed.

But remember, the whole dog is more important than his parts. Try not to focus too much on any one outstanding part, rather look at the dog as a whole. Even if several parts of the dog are outstanding, the dog will be worthless as a competitor if he lacks good balance, symmetry, and proportion.

Will my puppy's characteristics change?

Just about every trait a puppy possesses can change. Beautiful, plush puppy heads can turn into plain, poor adult heads. A long neck with smooth shoulders can turn into a short neck with heavy shoulders. A short-backed puppy can become a long-backed adult. A well-angulated rear can straighten.

Balance and symmetry

While these types of developmental changes do occur, it is extremely rare that a puppy's initial faulty characteristics correct themselves. An outstanding puppy has a much greater chance of developing into a good adult specimen than does a mediocre puppy.

Question the breeder about the typical developmental phases of the puppies. Breeders understand the unique maturation of their own bloodlines. For example, a breeder who has been working with one bloodline for a long time can easily select potential winners from that bloodline. Breeders know precisely what developmental changes to expect in their stock, and they know at what ages to expect those changes.

It's a different story, however, when breeders evaluate puppies from an unfamiliar bloodline. Then they must concern themselves only with the puppy's present appearance, not his future potential. This is because the developmental stages of different bloodlines follow different timetables.

When evaluating a litter of puppies, pick up each puppy and put it in a show stance – this is called "stacking" a puppy. This way the puppy's various traits can be seen, admired, faulted, and compared. This procedure also acquaints the puppy with the ritual of stacking and gives the puppy individual handling and attention. Stacking is necessary for an initial evaluation, but it is a common mistake not to go beyond it.

Should I "stack" a puppy to evaluate it?

The stacked position is unnatural to the dog, especially when carried to the extreme. Although a properly built dog will stack almost naturally, a dog that is not properly built can be manipulated to look better. Be aware that breeders may so skillfully manipulate a puppy in the stacked position that the dog will appear to be a better specimen than he actually is. For example, a breeder may pull the dog up and off the grooming table by his tail, swing his front legs out from under him, and tug on his tail so that he crouches and leans forward. By starting early with a young puppy, and by applying enough force and repetition, any dog can be manipulated into assuming the desired look in a stacked position.

Manipulative stacking does not change the dog's bone structure but it does create a false image of the dog. Not only does the ringside viewer see the false image, but the breeder/owner may also be deceived by his own adroitness at manipulating his dog. Sometimes the breeder has no idea that the dog loses his beautiful topline as soon as he leaves the stacked position. The breeder may truly believe that the dog is better than he actually is.

Therefore, when you are evaluating the puppies, pay close attention to how the puppies look on the ground without being stacked. The dog that deserves the most consideration will have a body that closely adheres to the breed standard, will carry his head proudly, will be well-coordinated, and will set himself up naturally. Pay special attention to how he uses his feet. A puppy that pivots easily and changes direction without looking awkward is generally put together well.

Terrier

Dogs who are the biggest winners in the show ring all possess one intangible quality. People have different names for it. Some call it heart, others call it soul, still others just call it showmanship. It is this quality that makes a judge select one dog over another, even if the dogs are of equal conformation.

What other qualities should I look for?

Sometimes a dog's conformation will leave you breathless when the dog is posed in a show stance. But put that same dog on the floor with the rest of the litter and he blends into the background. Then there's the dog who, when posed, could use a little more of this, a little less of that. But when this dog is on the floor, surrounded by other dogs, he draws attention to himself; he stands out from the crowd.

This is the kind of dog you are looking for: a dog that makes the most of what he has, a dog that possesses a superior personality, a dog that knows he is a winner.

It is this heart and soul quality that every top winner of every breed possesses. Without it, even a dog with superior conformation is "just another dog."

Most novices expect to be able to purchase a good dog from any breeder. A few blue ribbons and some puppy-match trophies can convince beginners that they are dealing with a successful breeder. Breeders who are not well-established may indeed produce good stock. However, they are not in a position to offer their best stock to others – they need it to improve their own bloodline.

From which breeder should I purchase my dog?

Buy your puppy from a successful, well-established breeder. Judge the breeder on objective criteria. Have this breeder's dogs finished their championships with good show records against good competition? Or did they finish against poor competition and take a long time doing so? Does this breeder sell good dogs to others or keep them? Are the breeder's dogs and their bloodlines in demand? Are the breeder's dogs producing quality lines? Do others breed their dogs to this breeder's dogs? You can find this specific information from breed books and by talking to exhibitors at dog shows. Also, breed magazines often publish lists of top-producing dogs and bitches based upon the number of champion offspring. They may also publish lists of top breeders.

Avoid the temptation to judge breeders on the size of their operations, on hearsay, or on information volunteered by the breeders themselves. Rather, judge individual breeders on the quality of their dogs.

Is is a good idea to form a relationship with a good breeder?

In order to form a relationship with a good breeder, you must first understand what drives him. Breeders want the best for their bloodlines. They also want their good dogs to be shown and to win.

Selling promising dogs to novices could be a bad move on the breeders' part. They could be unsure about novices' commitment to the dog game; they don't know if the novices will be able to raise their dogs properly or show them to their best advantage. As far as breeders know, novices could take "their" dogs and disappear from the face of the earth. A breeder puts a lot of heart, soul, and cash into producing a litter of puppies. Because the kennel name is on every puppy produced, the last thing a breeder wants is to let go of a promising puppy, especially to a novice.

If you demonstrate a high level of commitment to showing the dog, the breeder is more likely to offer a puppy of higher quality. Ways to prove your level of commitment include: discussing the possibility of engaging a professional handler to show the dog, allowing the breeder to guide you with regard to the puppy's upbringing, and letting the breeder have some say in the first breeding (for a female puppy). Work with the breeder to arrange terms that suit everyone.

Successful breeders are a fountain of knowledge because they have spent years breeding and raising dogs. They understand the art of breeding, they know the typical growth patterns of their bloodlines, they know how to raise puppies, and they know what makes a good dog. Further, most established breeders enjoy sharing this knowledge with the sincere, open-minded novice. Approach the breeder in a straightforward manner and ask for help and guidance. Breeders will teach the novice who really wants to learn.

Beware of choosing the wrong person to follow. When seeking the services of a doctor or lawyer, you look for one with a good professional reputation and avoid the quacks and shysters. When shopping for major purchases, you prefer brand names and quality in preference to the unknown and untried. Then, why would you select an unproved or less than adequate breeder as a mentor?

As a beginning breeder desirous of becoming a winner, you can understand that an experienced and successful breeder neither needs nor wants a "coat-tail crowd" or a group of "yes" men. Experience has made it possible for this breeder to discern fairly easily a novice worthy of his time and attention. As a newcomer, you are not expected to know it all and are expected to ask questions without feeling your questions will be regarded as silly.

Don't let fear that the big breeder will not want to bother with you make you think you should seek out second best, because any accomplishment looms large beside your own fumbling beginnings. To you, the neophyte, the word "champion" is truly the magic word – but remember, there are champions and there are CHAMPIONS.

There are many breeders, both successful and near successful, who are more than happy to lend a helping hand. They have usually reached their own pinnacle of success due to another's assistance along the way. Although successful breeders may help those they deem worthy, many not so successful ones may encourage associations with anyone willing. Gathering a group of disciples can provide a prop for an insecure ego, and it's not uncommon to find these breeders with their own personal retinues taking all they have to say as gospel. They pay little attention to the other dogs, rarely watch the judging with an objective eye so they can learn something, and have eyes only for the dogs belonging to their group.

You don't want to join such a coterie, because you don't want to become a second-rate breeder with very little true knowledge of your breed. Actually, you will have been used rather than helped. You will be tempted to remain in the fold by being made to feel obligated as a result of free stud services to the breeder's champion, gifts of dogs and special "deals." You realize that free stud services are not offered on good dogs, dogs are not given away that possess a monetary value and are in demand, and special deals rarely work out to everyone's satisfaction.

If you're not particularly careful, you'll quickly lose sight of your original goal of truly learning about dogs and becoming a winner.

How can I use this information to become my own person?

To be a good breeder you must be able to think independently and, when ready, begin to make your own decisions – to buy that puppy, to line-breed correctly, to keep that one great puppy. Learn all you can from your competent mentor and then go out and apply that knowledge.

This good advice puts me in mind of a real success story and one which I am proud to have had a guiding hand. Some years ago at the national specialty of the American Spaniel Club, I met a delightful couple, Tina and Al Blue, who, while not exactly in their 30s, were young and eager beavers in the breed. They had purchased a number of dogs from unrelated lines and had done some winning, but they felt they were just thrashing about with no real direction and no firm idea of what their "ideal" dog should look like.

After we had a number of interesting and stimulating conversations, they agreed that a knowledgeable and successful older breeder was the way to go. Fortuitously, they were able to meet Mrs. Ruth Mueller, a longtime breeder just longing to share her expertise. History was made. Among their top wins in a few short years was Best in Specialty show at the American Spaniel Club. I could cite dozens of other success stories just from my own personal experience.

You'll probably make some mistakes. Who doesn't? Remember though, you can learn as much from failure as you can from success. Study the dogs who are winning. Find out why and ask questions when you don't understand something. And, by all means, watch the judging and learn by observing where and how the judge places his hands, what he comes back to when he goes over a dog a second time. Many judges signal the ringside what they are looking for.

You have now located the ideal puppy to start you off in the dog game. Your excitement is great, your enthusiasm boundless. Then the breeder tells you the puppy's price. Before you accuse the breeder of overcharging, consider the following: breeders rarely make a profit on a litter of puppies, most merely hope to break even.

Why are purebred dogs so expensive?

There are many costs involved in producing and raising a litter: the stud fee, which can range from $100 to $500, based upon the dog's breed and the quality of the stud; shipping the bitch to the stud dog; veterinary exams and shots for all the puppies; additional food and vitamins for the dam (the mother of the litter); food for the puppies; and, advertising to sell the puppies. After all the expenses are paid and the puppies are sold, breeders feel fortunate if they make even a small profit.

Prices for show-quality puppies may range from $350 to $750, depending upon the breed, the bloodline, the puppy's age, and the region of the country. Before investing your dollars in a puppy, be sure to gather and evaluate information from individual breeders, other showdog owners, and the current and back issues of breed magazines.

The American Kennel Club (AKC) is a quasi-private corporation with a multi-million-dollar annual budget. It is run by delegates who are chosen by their local dog clubs. The delegates, in turn, elect a board of directors from their own ranks.

What is the AKC and its role in the governance of the sport of showing dogs?

Besides policy formulation and other standard business functions, the board hires a president, who functions as its chief executive officer, directing the staff and carrying out the policies of the board.

The major functions of the AKC:
- registering purebred dogs
- publishing the monthly Stud Book Register, which lists by breed the litters produced that month
- publishing a monthly journal, the *American Kennel Gazette*, which lists championship points earned by each dog, offers a wide variety of statistics about the status of the dog show game, month-by-month, and provides informative articles
- authorizing dog clubs as show-giving entities
- educating the public about purebred dogs
- sponsoring medical research of dogs
- sanctioning dog shows and approving dates and locations of shows
- licensing dog show judges
- overseeing shows
- representing the United States at international events that promote purebred dogs

To contact the AKC, write:
American Kennel Club
51 Madison Avenue
New York, New York 10010

For registration information:
American Kennel Club
5580 Centerview Drive
Raleigh, NC 27606

How do I register my puppy with the AKC?

The procedure is simple – the breeder will give you registration papers for the puppy. These need to be completed and mailed, along with a check in the prescribed amount, to the AKC. You will then receive a registration certificate from the AKC verifying that your dog is a purebred. This is an important document – you must use the registration number to enter your dog in an AKC show. This number will also be used to identify your dog in all subsequent breedings.

What are the benefits of joining a dog club?

When you join a dog club, you become a dues-paying member of the dog show world. You will meet people with similar interests, and make contact with breeders and exhibitors in your area. You will also have the opportunity to learn about dogs in general and about your breed in particular. And you may also have the opportunity to help organize and run dog shows in your area.

Local dog clubs are the backbone of the dog show world. The main goals of these clubs are to educate members and the public and to sponsor AKC-licensed dog shows. To sponsor AKC-licensed shows clubs must be given approval by the AKC, and they must hold the shows under AKC rules. Clubs must also select dog show judges from a list of AKC-licensed judges.

There are two kinds of local dog clubs: the all-breed club and the specialty, or breed, club. Specialty clubs focus on their individual breed, such as Collies or Pugs. For this reason, it is a good idea to join a specialty club if there is one in your area.

Local specialty clubs are under the jurisdiction of their national, or parent, club. And all dog clubs, local and national, are under the overall umbrella of the AKC. For example, the Southside Area Spaniel Club would be under the jurisdiction of the American Spaniel Club which, in turn, is under the jurisdiction of the AKC. A parent club is responsible for maintaining the official standard for its breed. All changes to a breed's standard must be approved by the parent club before being submitted to the AKC for final approval.

Congratulations! You are now the proud owner of a registered, purebred dog. You can now participate in the exciting world of exhibiting and breeding show dogs. But before you jump in head first, sit back and take a good, long look at your new puppy.

Your puppy depends on you for everything, so do your best to take care of him. Feed him properly, groom him, and make sure he receives veterinary care. But most of all, enjoy him. Keep in mind that your puppy is a living being first and a show dog second.

CHAPTER SUMMARY:

Understand your level of commitment.

Buy from a successful, established breeder.

Form a good relationship with the breeder.

Consider purchasing a male puppy.

Consider buying an older puppy.

Look for balance in the dog – get a total picture first.

Be aware that puppies change.

Look for the dog that sets himself up naturally.

Look for the showy dog.

Expect to pay a reasonable price.

The AKC registers purebred dogs, sanctions dog clubs and shows, licenses dog judges, and performs other tasks necessary to the sport of exhibiting and breeding purebred dogs.

Register your puppy with the AKC.

A specialty dog club is a great place to learn about your breed and to meet other exhibitors and breeders.

Enjoy your new puppy!

2 Form Follows Function

*"it has to be made right
to be right"*

If the only thing you learn from this book is that your dog has to be made right to do his designed job, then this volume has been a success.

The orginators of your breed, be it Weimaraner or German Wirehaired Pointer, had in mind certain features that allowed the dog the ability to do what they wanted from him. He was bred for a purpose. Dog breeds were specifically and painstakingly developed in their countries of origin to perform particular tasks. We will use the continental gun dogs of Europe as an example.

Editor Tony Jackson and his collaborators in their enlightening book, *Hunter Pointer Retriever* (HPR), state:

"The sporting nobility of Europe, with their vast estates and extensive variety of game required an all-purpose, one which could cope with differing terrain and game. Such dogs would be required to quarter the ground or close according to prevailing conditions, find game, staunchly point and on order flush, mark the fall and retrieve on command from land or water. The dogs would work not only on game and wildfowl but also boar and deer. Such breeds or types of dogs, the Hunter-Pointer-Retrievers, were thus developed with enormous skill and care.

"Continuing in this vein, each of the dogs (six in number) who make up the Continental Gun Dog family of HPR dogs has its own characteristics and that each is unique in appearance, conformation, color, type, style and method of working. Each has its own

---

Retriever

standard set in its country of origin, and as it has been imported into this country it has been registered and classified by the American Kennel Club. There is no reason at all why the structure of these breeds should be altered and it is essential to understand that one and the same dog can fulfill the necessary requirements for bench and field.

"You must take heed of the standard, without prejudice, since it is the blueprint based on the original prototype; those who know and understand how to read a pedigree (see Chapter 13) will be all too aware of the hazards of breeding the wrong type. For example, the correct coat is essential in a Gundog. No silky, thin, soft coat will stand up to punishing cover, a winter's day with the north wind biting or rain driving in sheets across the plain.

"The standards state that the German Shorthaired Pointer's coat must be short, flat and coarse, while the Hungarian Vizsla's coat is short, dense, coarse and greasy. The German Wirehaired has a distinctive coat which must be long and strong enough to protect the body. Its facial whiskers – a very particular feature – are intended to protect its eyes and mouth."

Each breed has a job to do and is specifically bred to do it in the most efficient way, from the Dachshund going to ground to the Bloodhound scenting along a trail, all are made to do a specific job. Once you understand the job, the structure of your breed takes on a more definitive meaning. AG

That form follows function is very important for you, as a breeder, to know. In many ways, it is a way to tell the differences in many breeds. Some examples:

Why is it important that I understand that "form follows function?"

- A Cocker Spaniel with its long neck allows the nose to be close to the ground so the long ears can help waft the scent of game.
- The galloping hunting hound has a unique physical form (a flexible spine, arched loin with somewhat sloping croup and low tailset and flat ribs) that follows the function, which is speed to run down game and/or kill or hold for the hunter.
- The Dachshund, whose function is to go to ground after game, which includes the dangerous badger,

Galloping Hound

has the form to perform such work (a long, low body, heavy bone and digging feet, and a long, powerful head and jaw).

If you have ever designed anything with functional parts, you know that structural design implies more than bare bones of anatomy. You know that a good design takes into account all factors that will help the structure serve its purpose. Similarly, the structural design of a dog must provide for all the needs of its owner.

In keeping with the principles of good architectural design, body and head structure must take into account the specific properties that the animal uses in his work. These materials must be able to withstand the stresses implicit in the design. Therefore, no breeder of a dog designed to herd flocks would think of placing a thin, unprotected skin where a tough layer of subcutaneous muscle and bristly coat should go. Here again, the inter-relationship of structure and function is obvious – the two go together.

How have form and function changed in today's dogs?

One of the most important things in designing and working with any breed is to keep in mind the inseparability of structure and function. That is, the form of the animal must be designed for the function for which it has been originally bred. Staying with this theme, the American Cocker Spaniel has some major structural problems that must be addressed if it is to perform as its originators desired. Cocker breeders have changed their standard to provide for a dog that is two inches shorter from withers to tail than from floor to withers. This creates a pretty, stacked dog but a badly engineered mover. Unless the shoulders are rotated far forward, the dog cannot get out of the way of its correctly designed rear. This causes the dog to step either inside or outside of his front legs, thus forcing him to sidewind down the ring. The American Spaniel Club has now changed the breed standard to correct this problem.

The function for which dogs were originally bred is not the function for which they are utilized today. Most Cockers are kept in a house or apartment as the family pet and seldom have the opportunity to demonstrate their specific skills.

What is the basis of breeds?

To go along with function, we have established breed types. These are based on physical forms that allow dogs to perform their functions and around which we weave artistic word descriptions. The definition of breed is type. The division of animals into groups of their species according to differences in physical types is the basis of breeds. A definite recognizable type must be common to all members of the group, for without breed type there is no breed. A breed is the highest form of a species. Over a number of generations of controlled breeding, certain dogs have developed definite physical characteristics that, taken together, are the consistent type of that species.

You can get a better understanding of the functional aspects of a breed of dog if you think of them in terms of engineering. Consider, for example, the role of the early breeders in England. They had two kinds of jobs. First, they tried to design a useful product: a dog who could go after upland birds, stay close to the hunter, have a good nose, be steady and have the ability to go all day long in the field. Originally, these hunting dogs had to put food on the table, only later were they used for sport.

What is organic engineering, as it pertains to dogs?

These early breeders had to find a way to manufacture these products. In bringing a new product into being, an engineer first lays out a method of operation. With the breeder, he might bring in another breed and cross it and re-cross it and introduce others until he got the correct mixture. The breeder might have to go through dozens of developmental stages before turning out a satisfactory replica of the designed product. No matter how many steps are necessary, a good product engineer (breeder) never departs from the intent of the basic design. He recognizes that the design has a special purpose which his efforts must serve. English farmers who had to protect livestock and fowl against foxes, who holed up in dens in rocky lairs, invented a sturdy little dog to take care of that problem.

This dog had to get along with the pack of hounds who were used to run the fox to ground. He needed a skull and ribcage that were flat enough to allow him to squeeze into any crevice the fox could. And finally, he had to have punishing jaws to kill the fox and haul him out. This little dog is now called the Lakeland Terrier. He is about the same size as a Cocker, but certainly built for an expressly different function.

But, whether we are talking about a dog breeder or an engineer, both design their products or devise techniques to make use of certain basic designs. For example, an engineer must use only those geometrical figures that would yield desired structural strength. He must also use shapes that will conserve on materials and yet provide for the greatest efficiency. Furthermore, he must also concern himself with simplicity of design.

A dog, or any living organism, is its own engineer. Throughout its life, it constantly refers to a basic design and manufactures the product it needs. In so doing, it makes use of the same principles of design that men use in building machines and other conveniences. The dog also makes use of the same mechanical principles that underline the operation of manmade devices. Consider, for example, the transmission of force. When an animal moves its moveable parts, it transmits force in much the same way that machines do. In so doing, the animal uses its built-in simple machines. This is why judging the gait of a dog in terms of its ability to perform its function is so very important in the overall approach to judging dogs.

How do dogs use energy?

For many years, physiologists and the majority of dog people believed that animals running at higher speeds would exact a higher cost in terms of energy burned, but it didn't turn out that way. Recent studies have shown that animals use up energy at a uniform, predictable rate as the speed of movement increases.

As if that shattering piece of information wasn't enough, they found out that for any given animal, the amount of energy expended in getting from point A to point B was the same, regardless of how fast the trip was taken. A Cheetah running 100 yards at a top speed of 60 mph, uses the same amount of energy as it would walking the same distance. The running is more exhausting because the calories are used up more quickly.

Size, however, does make a difference. Small dogs require much more energy per unit of weight to run at top speed than a Great Dane would. Small dogs appear to have higher "idling" speeds. The cost of maintaining muscular tension and of stretching and shortening the muscles are higher in small animals.

These same series of studies suggest that as much

as 77 percent of the energy used in walking comes, not from the operation of the muscles themselves, but from a continual interplay between gravity and kinetic energy. From an engineering standpoint, it seems that the body tends to rotate about a center of mass, somewhat like an egg rolling end-on-end or the swing of an inverted pendulum. The 30 percent of effort supplied by the muscles is imparted through the limbs to the ground to keep the animal's center of mass moving forward.

At faster speeds, four-footed animals appear to be capable of calling into use a work-saving scheme that relies upon the elastic storage of energy in muscles and tendons. Some are better at it than other, because some are capable of storing more energy per stride than others.

While running or trotting, the built-in springs for propulsion are the muscles and tendons of the limbs. When the animal has need to move even faster, he has the ability to use an even bigger spring. As dogs shift from a fast trot to a gallop, they tend to use their bodies as a large spring to store more energy. They do not change the frequency of their strides, rather they increase the length of them.

The dog can be compared to combinations of simple machines and other mechanical systems you might find in any factory. A few familiar examples will quickly clarify this analogy. The dog's legs could be diagrammed as levers. The appendages of all animals, in fact, serve as levers. If laid out side-by-side, they would present a rather special array of "machines." We have certainly seen dogs, from the Chihuahua to the Great Dane, present a wide variety of angles and levers.

How does the dog compare with man-made machines?

Modifications in such bio-levers reflect the animal's way of life. So, you would expect the Saluki's leg to be the kind of lever that gives the advantage of speed and distance; and by the same token, you would expect the design of the front legs of the Bassett, a burrowing animal, to be designed for multiplication of force, rather than for distance or speed.

Another simple machine that is easy to detect in

nature is the pulley. You'll find the living counterpart of the pulley wherever you find a muscle-tendon-joint apparatus. Whenever a tendon moves over a joint, it behaves like a pulley. Such mechanisms enable the dog to change the direction of force. A notable example of an application of the pulley principle is the action of the tendons and muscles in the dog's neck. When the handler strings the dog up on a tight lead, the ability of the dog to use that pulley correctly is gone.

Inclined planes are prevalent in all living things, but their presence is not always obvious. They frequently appear as wedges, which are made up of two inclined planes arranged back-to-back. The incisors of the dog, for example, are wedges. The cutting action of these teeth is an application of the wedge principle in nature. The terrier-type mouth is vastly different from that of the sporting dog. The sporting dog mouth is designed to hold a bird gently without crushing it. Therefore, its construction does now allow for great force to be generated. In contrast, the terrier jaws are punishing. They can generate enough force to kill game.

Another illustration is when a standard calls for a sloping topline in movement. The sloping plane from withers to tail is designed to harness the thrust or drive from the rear quarters and move the dog along a straight line with power.

Any person who has tried to dam up a creek or tried to manage moving water has had experience with hydraulics. Frequently, hydraulics deals with the transfer of mechanical energy of moving fluids to the powering of machinery. It also deals with the use of pressure created by fluids (hydraulic pressure). Applications of hydraulic pressure are evident in dogs. Certainly the pumping action of the heart as being responsible for the movement of blood through the circulatory system is an appropriate example.

A standard asking for a deep chest and a front wide enough for adequate heart and lung space is telling us room is needed for a pump big enough to keep the dog going under pressure all day long. If the heart is in need of repair or is worn out, the blood pressure of the animal varies abnormally. When this happens, the animal finds it hard to maintain a proper fluid balance of its tissues and organs.

A dog cannot function if the equipment designed to maintain hydraulic pressure fails. As you may recall from your school studies of anatomy, it takes more than the pumping of the heart to maintain normal fluid pressure in an animal. The condition of the arteries and the veins is equally important, for if these circulatory structures do not have the proper strength or elasticity, abnormal variations will develop in the hydraulic pressure of the body. Veins and arteries must have a structural design that will enable them to withstand and adjust to sudden changes in hydraulic pressure.

As the shape of a building usually reflects its function, so it is with the shape of the dog. In a large dog, the design often calls for a shape that will provide the necessary strength, compactness and capability to perform certain functions. For example, dogs such as the Husky are used to haul heavy loads. They were designed with a shoulder construction and balanced size that would enable them to perform this function. On the other hand, a long and slender shape characterizes speed required by the coursing type of dog (Afghan, Greyhound, Russian Wolfhound and Saluki). And then there is the Cocker, who is designed with a balanced shape to be neither a hauler or speed demon, but to go at a moderate pace for a sustained period of time.

How does shape relate to function?

Pulling Husky

What should I know about structure, shape and symmetry?

As we have noted, overall body shape has a definite relationship to a dog's way of life. Shape relates to the use of energy, to the ability to relate to environment, and to the function for which a dog was originally bred. As you continue to study dogs, you will see more and more how the shape of things facilitates function.

A major identifying characteristic of a breed is its head. The head and expression is the very essence of a dog, and without proper breed type and an individual is just a dog, not a Cocker, a Springer or even a Dane.

Balance is also very important. No part should be longer, shorter, larger or smaller than is compatible with the whole. Everything must fit together to form a pleasing picture of rightness.

Most breed standards call for a short back, and rightly so, for this is where the strength is. However, a short back is not synonymous with a short dog. The back is actually that small portion of the topline that lies between the base of the withers and the loin. A dog with a long, sloping shoulder and a long hip may give the impression of a longer dog. A dog that gives the impression of being taller than it is long is a dog badly out of balance, and this dog is quite likely to have such a short croup that it appears to have none at all. A short, steep croup will straighten the leg bones and lead to a highly ineffective and inefficient rear movement. A dog properly angulated at one end but not at the other is in even worse balance.

The upright shoulder is probably the worst imbalance of all because it affects every other part of the body. It puts great stress on a moving dog, making it pound its front feet into the ground, or crab sidewise to avoid interference with its hind feet.

As you look at your dog at home, in the show ring or out in the field working birds, look for the features of its design that might account for its survival and popularity. Look for the relationship of structural design to vital functions. Ask yourself, "How is this shape most suitable for the function of this structure; and, how is the body shape of this animal related to the environment in which it has to live?"

In searching for answers, go beyond the obvious facts and look for subtle relationships. Look for special problems. For example, in reading many of the breed magazines today, we find breeders bewailing the promiscuous breedings and the terrible things that have happened to their breed. They often point out their breed is no longer able to preform its primary function because of straight shoulders, over-angulated rears or too much coat. Their claim is the breed is no longer functional – form no longer follows function. What are the breeders of today going to do about it?

CHAPTER SUMMARY:

Dog breeders originally designed dogs to perform certain functions, such as hunting, herding, or protection. The functions for which dogs were bred determined their forms.

If breed standards are changed without respect to a breed's function, the results may produce an inferior breed.

You can get a better understanding of the functional aspects of a breed if you think of it in engineering terms.

Structure, shape, symmetry and balance relate to how well a dog functions in its environment and performs its duties.

Poodle on grooming table

Preparing Your Dog for the Show Ring

"critical impact time"

There is nothing more important to education than a positive attitude. If you want to be a winner you have to help your dog develop a positive attitude toward training and the eventual competition of the show ring.

Julie Daniels, in *Enjoying Dog Agility from Backyard to Competition* (Doral Publishing, Inc., 1991), points out that your dog's attitude toward new things has been shaped to some extent before now. He may approach physical challenges with delight, he may brave some novelties and fear others, or he may view anything new with misgivings.

Your dog's attitude is the first thing to consider each time you pick up the leash. What are your goals in this sport? What are you trying to accomplish with your dog today? How can you break that intermediate goal down into manageable progressions so you and your dog will become a better team for today's lesson.

If you don't feel relaxed about a certain training exercise, neither will your student, the dog. Either review a previously successful training exercise or train some other time, but don't let an introduction go badly.

Here are Julie Daniels' three basic guidelines for developing a positive attitude you and your dog need to get the most from your mutual education:

1. Attitude comes first, before the task is mastered. You are shaping attitude with guidance, correction or reward and with the feeling you project.
2. Begin your dog's training with challenges easier than you think he needs and progress only when your dog needs more challenge, not when you do.

Chapter 3. Preparing Your Dog for the Show Ring   ☐   27

A positive attitude toward the first training steps comes from quick early success. When you hit a real snag later on, leave that lesson alone for a week or so while you go back to the basics.

3. Chose your training time, enticements and challenges according to what best will strengthen your dog's educational foundation. Don't let someone else's timetable for progress dictate your own. Every dog learns unevenly and needs help differently.

So, think positive. It will make you a better handler and your dog a better partner. Take your time. A big problem with rushing any training is that it puts on pressure too soon, which undermines the happiness your dog feels for basic work.

Remember, an alert willing worker in the ring has an edge from the start. It's a definite plus in the judge's mind. AG

How can I prepare my dog for show?

Your dog will face many new experiences in the show ring, such as wearing a lead, posing in a show stance, gaiting, being handled by the judge, and seeing and smelling hordes of other dogs and people. You can help prepare your dog for the show ring by socializing him at an early age and by training him to pose, to wear a lead, to gait properly, and, for the smaller breeds, to feel comfortable while standing on a grooming table. A dog that is properly trained will be confident and comfortable in the ring.

The sections below briefly describe some of the ways to train a dog for the show ring. To obtain more detailed information, refer to one of the many books devoted to training and handling show dogs, such as *The Art of Handling Show Dogs* by Frank Sabella and Shirlee Kalstone (Hollywood: B & E Publications, 1980). You can also gather information from breeders and from fellow dog lovers at local club meetings.

When can I begin training my puppy?

Begin training your puppy as soon as you purchase him or, if you are the breeder, when he is weaned. The main goals of early training are to establish a loving relationship with your puppy and to develop the puppy's confidence. To accomplish these goals, work at a slow, steady pace, keeping in mind that

Socializing puppies early

baby puppies have short attention spans – just like human babies. First, try to understand the puppy's unique capabilities and limitations, then tailor the training sessions accordingly.

Socializing a dog – teaching him to be friendly towards people and other dogs – must also begin at an early age. A young puppy is so impressionable that the early socialization he receives will establish the foundation for his permanent personality. For this reason, remember to pet your puppy often, speak to him lovingly and reassuringly, and praise him frequently. Just as human babies thrive on tender loving care, so do puppies. As wee babies, they should be handled, petted, and loved. Never grab a puppy suddenly, lunge at him, or tease him.

How can I socialize my puppy?

Another important step in early socialization is to expose your dog to lots of people and other dogs. Try taking the dog to a public place, like a busy park, and let strangers pet him. Taking him to dog-show matches will also help him learn to be more comfortable in a crowd of other excited dogs and busy owners.

What should the first training sessions be like?

Following is a list of suggestions concerning the puppy's first training sessions. The main emphasis here is on love, respect, and on the puppy's distractibility and short attention span:

1. Hold the training sessions once a day at approximately the same time each day.
2. Make sure you and the puppy are both relaxed and ready to focus on training. If not, postpone the lesson.
3. Hold the first training sessions in a familiar, quiet place.
4. Begin with 10-minute sessions and gradually build up to 30 minutes.
5. Correct the puppy's mistakes in a gentle and firm manner, but never punish your puppy.
6. Praise and reward your puppy at the end of each training session.

How can I teach my dog to pose?

There are three steps involved in teaching a puppy to strike a "show pose:" familiarizing the puppy with the grooming table (see "What is a grooming table..."), teaching him to stand in a show pose, and training him to be handled by strangers while posing. None of these steps comes naturally to dogs, so be sure to use plenty of patience and tenderness while working with your puppy.

The first step in teaching a young puppy to pose is simply to let him become used to standing on a grooming table. Kneel down to the puppy's level and

Posing puppy

gently call him to you. Patting and praising him helps him feel secure and loved. Then, using both hands, carefully lift the puppy onto the table. He may squirm, so be sure to have a firm grip. Practice placing the puppy on the table one time during each training session until he seems comfortable, then move on to the next step.

The next step is to teach the puppy to pose. On the table, hold the puppy with your right hand under his chest and your left hand between his hind legs; at the same time, give the command "stay." If the puppy squirms, keep your hands in this same supportive position and gently lift his front feet off the table and set them down again; then, do the same maneuver with the hind feet.

Posing puppy

Repeat this rocking motion until the puppy settles down. Then, in order to teach him to support his own weight while holding a show pose, move your right hand up under his chin and your left hand up under his tail. Your puppy is now in a basic show pose. Keep in mind that the puppy may pull away or start squirming at any moment. Be ready to return quickly to the first position, with your hands supporting the puppy. When your puppy can maintain the posed position for one or two minutes, proceed with the next step.

The third and final step is to train the dog to hold the show pose while being examined by the judge.

Set your puppy in a show pose and have a friend – someone who is a stranger to the dog – check him over in the same manner that a judge will in the show ring. Have your friend check his teeth and bite, lightly feel his body, and, if your puppy is a male, check that the testicles are in place.

Once your puppy can hold a pose on the grooming table while being handled in this way, try posing him in a variety of other situations: on the lawn, in a park, or in a noisy room. This way, your puppy can become better acquainted with conditions that will more closely approximate a dog show.

When the puppy is old enough, another good way to teach him to pose is to enroll in a conformation class. These helpful classes are often offered by local dog clubs.

Training class

How can I train my dog to gait on a show lead?

The lead is one of the most important tools for all early training. We need our dogs to like the lead and to respect it. If a puppy dislikes his lead, it probably means that he associates being close to his handler (you) with not having fun. This we need to change. The first order of business is to build a good relationship between the dog and the lead.

Fig. 1. Gaits

Gently and slowly accustom your puppy to wearing a show lead. Starting at about six weeks of age, slip a soft collar on the puppy for five to ten minutes each day for a week or two. Your puppy will probably roll on the ground and try to remove the collar – so, stay with the puppy the entire time to make sure he does not injure himself. Afterward, praise and pat him, smiling and exclaiming what a good dog he is. Remove the collar after each training session so that the dog's neck hair won't wear away.

After the puppy becomes used to the collar, attach a show lead and let the puppy drag it around for about 10 minutes each day for several days. Don't hold the lead, just let the puppy wander freely. After a few days of this, take hold of the lead and allow him to take you for a walk. Once again, let the puppy wander wherever he wants. Do this for several days before trying to lead him. Remember: don't rush your puppy, and don't yank on the lead, or otherwise make the training sessions unpleasant. If you do, your dog could develop a lasting fear of the show lead.

Show lead

If your puppy doesn't like his lead, put it on him immediately before his favorite thing happens – supper, a ride in the car, a walk, a treat, a cuddle, a game of catch, etc. If a favorite person is coming to visit, put the lead on just before the door opens.

Once the puppy has become accustomed to dragging the lead around, the next step is to hold the lead and take the puppy for a walk. Here again, apply patience and gentleness in your approach, and limit lead training to no more than 10 minutes per session. Squat down to the puppy's level and say gently: "Speedy, come!" Then softly pull on Speedy's lead, just enough to start the puppy moving towards you. Praise your puppy when he comes to you, then move back several steps and repeat the sequence several times. It should not take long for the puppy to learn to follow you.

Once the lead is a friend, you can introduce some healthy respect. Any dog who spends his on-lead time straining to get further away from you is a dog who will not easily give up his freedom when off lead. Good lead work begins at home and then needs reinforcement away from home. If your puppy is very active, do this first exercise standing still. If he is more passive, you may want to start out walking, with frequent stops. Use a lead of about six feet long, kept loose. The idea is to teach your puppy to stay close enough to keep the lead slack at all times.

While a few, gentle dogs accept this readily if you pull them back or say a sharp NO! as soon as they begin to stray and then praise them for staying close, it's usually not this easy. Most dogs quickly decide that whoever pulls harder gets to go where he wants. These puppies need a different approach. You must jerk the lead as soon as he begins to take up the slack, and yank fast and hard enough to change his mind. Then praise him when he is paying attention again. Don't chastise the dog. If you jerk the lead early and strong enough to interrupt him effectively when he tries to charge off, you can quickly praise him when he is back to minding his manners.

To see that he learns to make the proper choice, use the lead to make him instantly uncomfortable when he tries to take off, and use your voice to make him instantly pleased with himself when he changes his mind. It does no lasting good to hang on tight, since that causes him to pull away. It takes two to pull. Help the puppy decide for himself to stay close so it becomes a habit and further training can proceed.

At first, teach the puppy to gait on your left, later teach him to gait on your right. By switching sides often, your puppy is less likely to develop a problem with sidewinding. (Sidewinding can occur if the puppy's hind legs are trying to move faster than his forelegs, causing the hind legs to wind around on one side of the dog.)

Each time you stop moving, teach the puppy to stop also and to stand alertly in a natural pose. Don't hand pose your puppy during lead training. Keep posing and lead training separate. Otherwise, the puppy may expect you to pose him each time you stop moving, and may not learn to pose himself naturally.

If your puppy sits each time you stop walking, try this: just as you are about to stop, distract him with a squeaky toy or a piece of food while you continue to take a few steps forward. Or, if this doesn't work, put your toe under his hindquarters to prevent him from sitting. In case this method also fails, and as a last resort, tie a rope around his belly and have a friend hold him in a standing position when you stop walking. After your puppy has mastered the fundamentals, switch to a one-piece show lead or, for larger dogs, to a choke chain.

Teach your puppy to move forward, turn, and then walk back to the starting position in a straight line. Next, practice all the different movement patterns used in the show ring: circles, "Ls," "Ts," and triangles. Practice gaiting on various surfaces, such as grass, concrete, and rubber mats (these are used at indoor shows).

Hold the lead loosely when teaching your puppy to gait; this will help the puppy to carry himself naturally. Often, a judge will ask you to "take the dog up and back on a loose lead." If the puppy has always been gaited on a tight lead, he could learn to depend on this extra support and may drop his head when gaited on a loose lead: the dog's natural carriage and

Fig. 2. Show Patterns

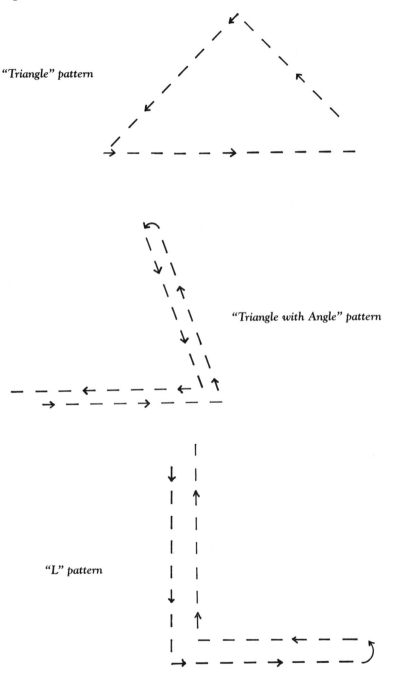

"Triangle" pattern

"Triangle with Angle" pattern

"L" pattern

topline will then be gone. In addition, he may also develop a problem with sidewinding. If your puppy is taught to gait on a loose lead, he will develop his natural carriage and gait proudly with his head up.

Determine the proper gait for your dog. Commonly, novices will walk their dogs too slowly in the ring. If the dog is small, the handler should be walking at normal speed. If the dog is medium or large, the handler should be walking quickly or trotting. However, if your dog has a short back, don't move too quickly: this may cause your dog to sidewind in an effort to keep up. Be sure that you move with long, smooth strides when showing your dog; these strides look more graceful and will hold the judge's attention on your dog, not on you. As a general rule, do not race around the ring; go at a pace that's comfortable for your dog. Remember, every dog, even of the same breed, is built somewhat differently, so practice and use the gait best for that particular dog.

A very good way to know how your dog looks to the judge, and to practice gaiting and posing properly, is to use full-length mirrors. Especially keep an eye on the dog's topline and single tracking (legs coming toward a single center line as speed increases). It is also important to see which head and neck position enhances the dog's topline.

How can I get my puppy used to being in a crate?

Show dogs spend a lot of time in their crates. They are transported to and from shows in them, and, when not in the ring, they usually stay in their crates during the show. If properly acquainted with the crate, a dog can come to feel that the crate is his own special haven.

You will want to introduce the crate to your puppy at an early age. To begin with, put a small treat in the crate, and place it on the floor near the puppy's water bowl. At first, your puppy will probably stay as far away from the crate as he possibly can. After a few hours, however, curiosity will get the better of him and he will snatch the tidbit. To encourage familiarity with the crate, replace the goody several times a day. After a week or so, your puppy should become more comfortable with the crate.

Puppies in crate

The next step is to place the puppy gently in the crate, with a tidbit inside, and gently shut the door. Leave the puppy in the crate for 10 minutes or so, offering another treat if necessary. Most likely, the puppy will whine and fuss about being locked up; stay in the room with him the entire time, providing assurance and comfort with a soft voice. Then, after 10 minutes, let the puppy out of the crate and praise him lavishly for being such a good sport. Over the next few weeks, gradually build up the time until the puppy accepts a few hours of confinement as natural.

Your puppy should now be ready to sleep in his crate every night. But, remember that a small puppy has a small bladder; be sure to let him out of the crate early in the morning.

Once this goal has been reached, you will want to begin training your puppy to travel in his crate in the car. Begin with a 10-minute trip and gradually build up to an hour or so. Be aware that puppies can easily become car sick; speak soothingly to him and return home quickly if he begins to feel ill.

What is a grooming table and why do I need one?

A grooming table raises the dog to your working height for grooming and training. In addition to saving your back from potential straining, the grooming table helps establish rapport between dog and master. Even though the young puppy on a training table is facing a new, potentially frightening situation, he is comforted by the presence of his master, and the bond of trust is strengthened.

Early table training is advantageous in other ways as well. It teaches the dog to be relaxed while being groomed on the table, and it makes "posing training" easier, since it is easier to control a young puppy on a table than on the ground.

When selecting a grooming table, look for one that is sturdy and has a nonslip surface. In addition, there are several other features to be aware of when purchasing a grooming table. For example, some tables are portable and/or adjustable, and some are a combination crate and grooming table.

One optional feature of most grooming tables is the post and loop collar. This collar is used to hold up the dog's head, preventing him from squirming and/or jumping off the table. If you decide to purchase a table with a post and loop collar, do not use a collar with choking action; and, never leave your puppy alone on the table, especially if his head is in the loop. If you are unsure what grooming table features you might want, talk with other owners of dogs like yours to determine what works best for your breed of dog.

Where can I learn to groom my puppy?

To learn how to groom and trim your dog for a show, take your puppy to a professional dog groomer who knows or specializes in your breed, or to the breeder from whom you purchased the dog, and observe and learn the groomer's techniques. Before showing the dog, bathe him, make sure his nails are clipped, and then trim, comb, and brush his coat.

Some breeds, such as Doberman Pinschers,

require docked tails, cropped ears, and dew claw removal. Check the breed standard and your local dog club for helpful information about specific show ring requirements for your particular breed.

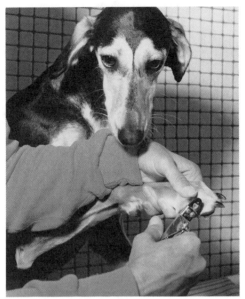

Proper nail clipping

CHAPTER SUMMARY:

The main goals of early training are to establish a loving relationship with your puppy and to develop the puppy's confidence and personality.

Work at a patient, gentle pace when training a puppy to pose and gait, and when acquainting him with the lead, the crate, the car, and the grooming table.

To learn how to groom and trim your dog for a show, first take your dog to a professional dog groomer, or the dog's breeder, and observe and learn the groomer's techniques.

Understanding How Dog Shows Work

An old saying has it that the proof of the pudding is in the eating. How true. And the proof of your dog's ability to win will be proved in the show ring. That said, don't believe that the best dog will always win. Too many factors go into the brief appearance your dog makes before the judge to make it a certainty that the "best" dog will win.

Picture a large class of 20 dogs at a typical, large show. The judge has about two and one-half minutes per dog to arrive at his decision for that day. Unless your dog goes into the ring like gangbusters and catches the judge's eye early, his chances of winning are diminished.

This means you must understand before you go into the ring just what this event is all about so you can make the best of your talents as well as those of your dog. You've got to understand what the scheme of a dog show is all about, the importance of doing the little things right, like being at ringside on time and studying the judge in previous classes to see how he moves his dogs and manages the ring, then give him what he wants to see – in spades.

A very important point is "don't get beat before your dog goes into the ring." Show grounds are often rife with rumors: Ch. Whooziz has a lock on Best in Show today. If anyone thought to ask why, the most likely response would be they say so, and if traced down who they were, and why they thought that way, you would probably find out that an exhibitor or handler commented to another that Judge Dingbat gave old Whooziz a long look in the Group two months ago.

Little voices took it from there and parlayed it into a sure thing. Just remember that racetrack handicappers equipped with better information are right less than 50 percent of the time, and don't be dismayed by those rumors that go so far as to which class dog will win.

Also, as you wander around before your scheduled time in the ring trying to sight your class competition, remember, many of them can look like world beaters on the grooming stand. However, you're going to beat them down on the ground and moving. Don't panic and think they are all better than your dog. They are not! AG

What are the different types of dog shows?

Dog shows will be a whole new way of life. You will be exposed to sights and sounds and terms that may confuse your senses at first. Just remember that dog shows are set up somewhat similarly to the NCAA final basketball tournament. There is Breed competition (dogs of the same breed), which is like the preliminary rounds of play in a tournament. In this example, the best dog in each of some 130 breeds is selected to go on to compete in the next higher round, the Group competition. You can liken this to a combination of the quarter and semifinal rounds.

The groups are basically clustered by function. Cocker Spaniels, Pointers, Springers, Golden Retrievers, etc., make up the 24-dog Sporting Group – all of which hunt and retrieve birds and other small game. Collies, Shelties, Corgis, etc., make up a group of dogs with herding responsibilities, so they are in the Herding Group. In all, there are seven groups.

Each group is judged by an AKC-licensed judge who is knowledgeable on dogs within that group. His job is to select the "best" dog to go on to compete in the seven-dog final round for the Best in Show award. The final lineup is like the final four and championship game all rolled into one. The eliminations are over and only one of the seven finalists can emerge as the Best in Show. There is no semifinal or playoff for third place. The dog selected for Best in Show wins all the marbles.

For you, the most important action will take place in your breed ring. This is where all of your attention needs to be focused and where you will spend 90 percent or more of your time at dog shows.

The breed ring is where you need to learn breed type and soundness. You can't do it by going to one show or even 10. It comes from intelligent observation and by understanding what the breed standard really means. Your breed standard is usually only about two or three pages long, but it is packed with relevant information. Each time you read a part of the standard, i.e., shoulders well laid back, ask why? By doing this you can begin to find out that dogs are built around the tasks they were designed for. Then, and only then, will the standard make sense to you.

The AKC, in cooperation with your national breed club, has put together a video on your breed standard. Be sure to get a copy. They may be obtained for $35 by writing: AKC Videos, 51 Madison Ave., New York, NY 10010.

In addition, there are usually one or more books about your breed available. Buy one (preferably one published by Doral) and study it for a picture of the breed as it has developed over the years. Do not buy the $5.95 books found in pet stores. All they contain are some pictures and very general information that will not further your cause.

Back to the breed ring! Watch the judge sort out his winners and then ask yourself why he did that. Record your answers as well as the name and date of the show. After doing this for 10 shows, look at your reasons for the judges' actions. Are you beginning to see a rationale for their decisions? You should. If you think it's all politics or the judge is crooked, you are off on the wrong track and are probably listening to too many disgruntled losers. Start again and form your own opinions by understanding why you've reached your conclusions. Then begin to discuss them with other serious breeders/exhibitors.

There are three types of conformation dog shows: all-breed shows, specialty shows, and matches. Each type of show serves a different purpose.

All-breed shows are sponsored by all-breed clubs.

As indicated by the name, all AKC-approved breeds may be exhibited at an all-breed show. AKC championship points are awarded to Winner's Dogs and Winner's Bitches. For more information about championship points, see the section entitled "How does a dog become a champion?"

Specialty shows are sponsored by specialty clubs and are the most prevalent type of dog show in the country. Any breed club that is licensed by the AKC may sponsor this type of show. Only a single breed, such as Brittany or German Shepherd Dogs, is exhibited at a specialty show; this makes the competition for points intense. Championship points are awarded to Winner's Dogs and Winner's Bitches. Naturally, exhibitors consider winning at a specialty show to be a significant event.

The third type of show is the match. There are both all-breed and specialty matches. Most of these are held under AKC sanction, but no championship points are awarded to the winners. Matches provide a practice ground for novice exhibitors, experienced breeders breaking in their newest show prospects, dog clubs working to become approved by the AKC, and prospective judges who want to become licensed by the AKC. This type of show is fun to attend; it's a great place to learn how to exhibit your dog, and for the dog to learn proper ring manners.

What are the different competitive classes?

Dog shows, like most sporting events, classify the competitors by age, sex, and experience at winning. For example, in golf, competitors are classified by sex, age (seniors, juniors), and by professional/amateur status. At dog shows, dogs trying to earn their championships compete by gender within the following six classes:

• Puppy, 6 to 9 months
• Puppy, 9 to 12 months
• Novice – open to dogs that have not yet won a class
• Bred-by-Exhibitor – open to dogs being shown by their breeder (who must also be their current owner)
• American-Bred – open to dogs bred in America
• Open Class – open to all dogs, including puppies

Dogs that have already earned their championships are entered directly into the Best of Breed or Best of Variety competition. This option is only available to AKC champions.

Specialty shows will sometimes include the class: "Puppy, over 12 months and under 18 months."

Every breed is judged in the same way. First, the male "Puppy, 6 to 9 Month" class is judged. The judge selects the top four puppies and awards them first, second, third, and fourth places. The judge then proceeds through the rest of the regular classes, ranking the top four males in the "Puppy, 9 to 12 Month" class, the Novice class, the Bred-by-Exhibitor class, the American-Bred class, and, finally, the Open class.

How does a dog show work?

Next, the first place winners from each of the classes are brought back into the ring to compete against each other in the Winners class. From this competition, the judge selects the Winners Dog; this is the only male of this breed who will receive championship points at this dog show. The second place dog of the original class in which the Winners Dog was entered is then brought into the ring to compete against the other class winners for the title of Reserve Winners Dog. If for any reason the Winners Dog is later disqualified, the Reserve Winners Dog will receive the championship points – this, however, is a rare occurrence.

This entire process is then repeated for the female dogs, culminating in the selection of a Winners Bitch and a Reserve Winners Bitch – the Winners Bitch being the only female of this breed who will receive championship points at this show.

Next comes the Best of Breed or Best of Variety competition. All the AKC champions (male and female), as well as the Winners Dog and the Winners Bitch, are brought into the ring to compete for the Best of Breed award. From this assembly, the judge selects the Best of Breed winner. The judge then compares the Winners Dog and the Winners Bitch, and selects one of them to be the Best of Winners. If either the Winners Dog or the Winners Bitch was named Best of Breed, that dog automatically becomes the Best of Winners as well. Next, the judge selects a Best of Opposite Sex to the Best of Breed. That is, if a male was selected as Best of Breed, the judge will select a female to be Best of Opposite Sex, and vice versa.

If the number of championship points awarded to the defeated class Winner is greater than those awarded to the Best of Winners, then the Best of Winners will automatically receive the same number of points as the defeated Winner. For example, suppose that four points are awarded to the Winners Bitch, but only two points are awarded to the Winners Dog. If the Winners Dog is subsequently named Best of Winners, he will receive four championship points, not two. Of course, the Winners Bitch will still receive four points as well.

Some breeds have no Best of Breed competition at all-breed shows; instead, they are subdivided into different varieties that compete independently for championship points in a Best of Variety competition.

For example, American Cocker Spaniels are separated into three varieties based on coat color: Black, Parti-Color, and ASCOB (Any Solid Color Other than Black). These varieties compete independently from each other, as though they were completely different breeds. Thus, instead of one Best of Breed competition for the breed as a whole there are three separate Best of Variety competitions (in Specialty shows the Variety winners compete against each other for a Best of Breed award), and six American Cocker Spaniels will earn championship points at each show: the Winners Dog and Winners Bitch of each variety.

In an all-breed show the winners of each Best of Breed and Best of Variety are brought together in a group competition. There are seven groups: Sporting, Hound, Working, Terrier, Toy, Non-Sporting, and Herding. The top four dogs are selected in each group but only the first place winner continues on in the competition. See Appendix for a list of all breeds by group.

Finally, the seven group winners compete in the Best in Show competition, from which the top dog is selected. At some of the larger shows up to 3000

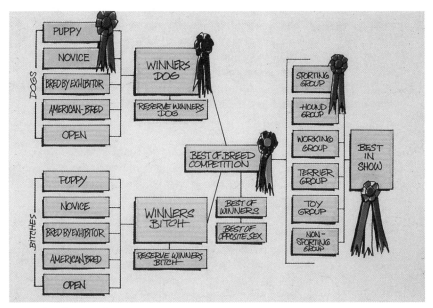

How a dog show works

dogs may be evaluated and ranked over the course of one day.

Up to five championship points are awarded at AKC dog shows to the Winner's Dog and Winner's Bitch of each breed. Shows are considered majors for a given breed if three, four, or five championship points are to be awarded. A dog must earn 15 championship points to become a champion. The AKC has established the following requirements for the way the points must be earned:

How does a dog become a champion?

- The dog must earn points under at least three different judges.
- The dog must earn points from at least two major wins.
- The major wins must be under at least two different judges.

Only dogs that are not already champions compete for points. Your dog need not be the best of his breed to earn points; he only needs to be the best among the nonchampions of its sex.

AKC statisticians calculate the number of points to be awarded by considering several factors: the number of dogs of the same breed and sex competing at that particular show, the popularity of the breed, the geographical region of the show, and the number of dogs that were shown in that region last year. The schedule of points to be awarded at a show are published in the show's catalog.

Who are the various officials at dog shows?

Many people are needed to run a dog show: the show chair and show committee; the show superintendent; ring stewards; judges; and an AKC field representative.

The "show chair" is a member of the dog club sponsoring the show. This person is responsible for running the show and, as such, performs many duties before, during, and after the event. Some of these duties include: employing the show superintendent, judges (usually with the help of a committee), ring stewards, the show photographer and sanitary engineers; reserving and preparing the show site; making certain all the judges have arrived and have been provided with rooms and meals; seeing that ribbons and trophies are at the proper rings; arranging for food service; making certain that the show site is properly cleaned up after the show; and, contacting the AKC with the results of the show.

The "show committee" consists of members of the local dog club who assist the show chair with running the show. They also handle complaints about infractions of rules and, if justified, hold disciplinary hearings at the show.

A "show superintendent" is typically an independent manager hired by a dog club to organize and manage a show. Show superintendents are usually responsible for the secretarial functions of a dog show: publishing and mailing show announcements and premium lists; taking entries of dogs for the show, including collecting entry fees, scheduling the show rings, and sending each exhibitor and judge a packet of information about the show.

"Ring stewards" are typically either members of a professional steward association, or are volunteers from the local dog community. They are responsible for organizing and running a given ring. Their duties include: handing out a numbered arm band to the each exhibitor about a half hour before his dog is to be shown; announcing which class is showing next; making sure that the entered dogs arrive in the ring at the proper time; informing the judge which dogs are absent; arranging ribbons and trophies so they're ready for the judge to hand out; recording the results of judging; and, generally keeping the ring's activities on schedule.

"AKC field representatives" are present to oversee compliance with all AKC rules and regulations.

"Judges" must fully understand the breed standards for all the breeds they are judging. They are expected to evaluate and rank up to 175 dogs per day (excluding groups and best-in-show), at the rate of 20 to 30 dogs per hour. Judges usually award ribbons to the best four dogs in the ring. However, sometimes a judge may feel that no dog is worthy of an award; and, in this rare instance, the judge may decide to withhold awards.

Prospective judges have usually been successful breeders or professional handlers for many years; at a minimum, they must have been in the dog show game for 10 years and bred four litters and two champions. When they apply for AKC judges' licenses, they must: complete comprehensive questionnaires about their involvement with the dog show world; visit with breeders of the breed they wish to judge; take written tests on the breeds they wish to judge; be interviewed by an AKC field representative; and, they may have to take a "hands-on" test, judging a preselected class of eight dogs while being evaluated by two judges and an AKC field representative.

How do judges become licensed by the AKC?

Once they have passed these hurdles, their names are published in the American Kennel Gazette, the monthly magazine of the American Kennel Club. Persons having knowledge of these candidates may write to the AKC either for, or against, them. Finally, an AKC panel reviews and analyzes the overall qualifications of the prospective judges. Using prescribed guidelines, the panel grants – or denies – a candidate the license to judge one or more breeds.

The candidate must go through similar subsequent applications in order to judge additional breeds.

Once granted the AKC license to judge an initial set of breeds, fledgling judges must judge each of these initial breeds at least five times before they can apply for other breeds. During this period, they are known as provisional judges. Their actions are monitored carefully by AKC field representatives and reports are written on their ring procedures and on their general knowledge. Even after being granted status as a regular judge, all judges are periodically evaluated by the AKC and a report is submitted both to the individual judge and to the AKC.

How can I learn more about my breed?

To learn more about your breed, we suggest you subscribe to your breed magazine. The names of all breed magazines can be found in The Canine Source Book (Bulanda, Doral Publishing, 1990). In addition, there are a number of general magazines and newspapers that cover all breeds and provide an overview of the dog scene. They are:

Kennel Review
11331 Ventura Blvd, #301
Studio City CA 91604
$55 per year (10 issues plus giant Xmas annual)

Dog Watch
11311 Ventura Blvd, #301
Studio City CA 91604
$120 per year (weekly)

American Kennel Club Gazette
51 Madison Ave
New York NY 10010
$24 per year (12 issues)

D, The Dog Magazine
Harris Publications
1115 Broadway
New York NY 10160-0397
$60 per year (8 issues sent first class)

Dog News
Harris Publications
1115 Broadway
New York NY 10160-0397
$57.97 for 25 issues (weekly)

Dog Fancy
PO Box 6040
Mission Viejo CA 92690
$21.97 per year (12 issues)

Bloodlines
United Kennel Club
100 East Kilgore Road
Kalamazoo MI 49001-5598
$12 per year (bi-monthly)

Good Dog
PO Box 31292
Charleston SC 29417
$12 per year (6 issues)

Canine Chronicle
605 Second Avenue North, # 203
Columbus MS 39701
$80 per year

Dog World
29 N Wacker
Chicago IL 60606-3298
$24 per year

CHAPTER SUMMARY:

There are three types of dog shows: all-breed shows, specialty shows, and matches. AKC championship points are awarded at all-breed shows and specialty shows. Matches provide a practice ground for novice exhibitors, breeders, judges, and dog clubs.

Dogs are shown in different competitive classes: Puppy, Novice, Bred by Exhibitor, American Bred, Open Class, and Best of Breed/Best of Variety. Eighty-five percent of all Winners dogs and bitches come from the puppy classes or the Open Class.

To become a champion, a dog needs to earn 15 AKC championship points in the show ring.

Judges generally have many years of experience in the dog show world, and they must conquer many hurdles in order to obtain and keep AKC licenses to judge.

PART II
EXHIBITING

5

Showing Your Dog

"jumping in the deep end"

Practice is over. Now is the time for the real thing. You're confident that your dog's attitude reflects his training and confidence in himself and in you. Now you both want to try your wings. Taking him to a match show for his initial flight into the show world is probably the best first step. There is less chaos and more time to visit and socialize for both of you – and the competition shouldn't be as tough.

At this point, stage fright is a real possibility. The informality of a match show will help both of you surmount that hurdle. Remember, an important part of showing is to show the dog to his maximum advantage. This means you stay in the background and let the dog do his thing to the best of his ability. This also means that you shouldn't handicap your dog by stringing him up on the lead so tightly that he barely has his front feet on the ground and has no control of his neck and shoulders. His head may be high, but he will look like a spastic alligator. Train and show your dog on a semi-loose lead so he can show to the best advantage. AG

Before entering your dog in a show, you must register the dog with the AKC. Please refer to Chapter 1, under the section entitled "How do I register my puppy with the AKC?" for a review of this topic.

How do I sign up my dog for a show?

You can learn about upcoming dog shows through your dog club, in dog magazines (including the

American Kennel Gazette), and by mailings. To sign up for a particular dog show, simply complete and mail in the entry form and fee (typically $15 to $20 per dog) by the deadline. Once you are on a dog show superintendent's mailing list (and your name may stay on that list forever), you will receive announcements by mail for all that superintendent's shows. A list of all show superintendents may be found in *The Canine Source Book* (Bulanda, Doral Publishing, Inc., 1990).

Most dog shows require entry at least three weeks before the show, but sometimes dogs may be entered in a match on the day of the show. The entry form will require the dog's registered name and number, birthdate, sex, names of both sire and dam, and the names of the breeders and the owners. You will also need to select a class in which to exhibit your dog. (See Chapter 4, "What are the different competitive classes?") Generally, as you get to know what it's all about, you'll find it's best to skip the Novice and American-bred classes. My personal preference is Bred-by-Exhibitor, if you've bred the dog.

You will soon receive a packet of information from the show superintendent containing: directions to the show site; a form noting which ring and what time your dog is to be shown; a list of the judges assigned to this particular dog show and to your breed; and, an exhibitor's pass which will allow you free entrance into the show.

What supplies should I take to the show?

Assemble and pack in your car, van or RV the following items:

- the registration packet mailed to you by the show superintendent, including your exhibitors pass and a map to the show site
- a road map
- sunglasses, sunscreen, and hats with visors, if necessary
- your dog's crate, lined with newspaper
- your dog's regular food, food bowl, and water bowl
- a quart or two of fresh water
- a show lead
- a portable grooming table, if you use one and think you would like it at the show

- all the grooming supplies you normally use
- treats and toys for your dog
- a pooper scooper
- a portable exercise pen
- folding lawn chairs.

You'll also want to pack a picnic lunch, or plan to purchase lunch at the show. You will also need cash to cover parking fees and miscellaneous items commonly for sale at dog shows. Also, be sure to wear comfortable walking shoes.

Carolyn Anderson, a fashion professional writing in the Spring 1991 issue of *Brittany World*, points out that a dog show is a theatrical event and, as such, the handler is the backdrop for the dog. The judge eyes the dog in front and beside the handler. Attire should complement the dog, never overpower him. The judge should see the dog and not be distracted by the handler's wardrobe.

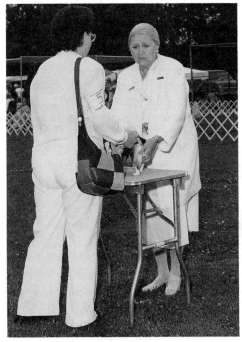

Is this purse necessary?

Color is one of the most important aspects of dressing for the show ring. Royal blue, navy, turquoise, teal green and other colors in that family are excellent choices. Yellow and some shades of orange also work well.

Anderson tends to refrain from red and burgundy but indicates that they would be wonderful colors if showing a liver-colored dog; shades of purple and lavender should work equally well. White is a color to be avoided at all times because it would compete with the white in a dog's coat. Off-white, creme and shades of tan and khaki are acceptable.

Women should avoid large prints, florals and especially large plaids (men: no large, bright plaid sportscoats) as they tend to compete with dogs that are liver, orange and white. Glen plaid and small prints work as long as they have the effect of being a solid color.

Being well dressed in the show ring is not going to insure victory, but it will demonstrate a sense of pride in your dog and his accomplishments. It will give you as handler a sense of self-confidence in knowing that you look good and that self-confidence will be felt by your dog.

Now you should be ready to go – just fill your thermos with steaming hot coffee and take off down the highway.

Oh, and don't forget King Ferdinand IV!

How do I take care of my dog on an overnight trip?

If you need to travel quite a distance and stay overnight in a motel, make certain that your dog is allowed in the room with you. You may want to make these arrangements by telephone before your trip. Also, plan to eat dinner in your motel room, unless you're confident that your dog will not howl and cry while you're away; this would be upsetting and unfair not only to the dog, but also to the other motel guests. Don't groom or bathe your dog in the room and clean up after your dog when exercising him. Leave the premises the way you found them to be a good neighbor.

While travelling in your car, stop every few hours to let your dog drink water, exercise, and relieve himself. Most highway rest areas have large grassy spaces designated for leashed pets. These rest breaks are also a good time to stretch your legs and check your map.

At your first show, you may feel as though you're surrounded by chaos: barking dogs; exhibitors madly grooming dogs that are already beautiful; the smell of hamburgers, hotdogs, and french fries; announcements blaring over the loudspeaker; rows of vendors hawking their wares – everything from collars to dog books to flea spray; folks with serious, intent frowns, and others with beaming grins; children running here and there; and, badge-bearing, clipboard-carrying officials strutting from one ring to the next. But, perhaps the most amazing sight are the hordes of dogs, the likes of which you have never imagined!

What can I expect at my first show?

Vendors hawking wares at dog show

You will see rare breeds, such as Otter Hounds, Portuguese Water Dogs, American Water Spaniels and Brussels Griffons. You will see dogs with exotic names, such as Salukis, Pharoah Hounds, Borzois, and Basenjis. You'll meet enormous walking dustmops, Komondorok and Pulik. And, if you've never met an Irish Wolfhound, you're in for quite a shock – these giants stand almost three feet high at the shoulder.

They could actually place their paws on your shoulders and look you square in the face.

Before you and your dog become overwhelmed by the commotion, make your way to the grooming area. Here you can set up your dog's crate and pen, grooming table and supplies, folding chairs, picnic lunch, and such. About 30 minutes before your dog's scheduled show time, go to the ring where the dog will be shown and pick up your exhibitor's arm band from the ring steward.

Grooming area

How do I handle my dog in the ring?

Before you actually enter your assigned ring, it's a good idea to observe the judge. Watch how he lines up the dogs, trots them around the ring, and goes over them. Perhaps this judge likes dogs to move up and back or move diagonally across the ring. Once you understand the judge's preferences, you can mentally prepare to execute the same moves with your dog.

To impress the judge, enter the ring promptly and have your dog ready to show. Now and then an exhibitor is delayed in another ring; this is understandable, and the judge generally gives wide latitude to make sure all entries will be exhibited.

(This is because more entries in the ring will yield more championship points to the Winners Dog and the Winners Bitch.) However, a judge cannot keep the ring waiting indefinitely (the AKC expects judges to go over 25 dogs per hour), so it is important that you always have a substitute handler available to show your dog, if necessary.

As you enter the ring, make sure your arm is pivoted towards the judge and steward so they can read the entry number on your arm band. Now take a deep breath and relax!

Yes, most judges are impressed with expert handling and good grooming of both the dog and handler, but this alone will not automatically win any awards for your dog. But, the judge will notice that you care enough to present your dog at his best. Keep in mind that your dog is a winner and so are you, no matter what the judge decides. Everybody loves a winner, and judges are no exception.

Judges usually start off the judging by having the handlers move the dogs around the ring; simply stay in line and keep pace with the other handlers. Be sure to pay close attention to the judge; sometimes he will want to rearrange the order. To do this, a judge will typically point to a handler and signal him to step out of the line. Usually the judge will also indicate where the handler should wait.

Next, judges will usually line the dogs up for inspection. Make certain that your dog is positioned directly in line with the other dogs. Place your dog in a show pose and have your dog hold the pose until inspected by the judge, unless otherwise instructed. As the judge is examining your dog, hold onto the dog's muzzle until the judge inspects his head. Later, when the judge begins to place his hands on the dog's head, let go of the head and place your index and middle fingers just behind the dog's skull so that he can't pull his head back.

If your dog has hanging ears, hold them up towards his nose when the judge is inspecting his neck and shoulders, and also when the judge is viewing the dog from behind – this affords the judge a better view of the dog. Remember to stand on the opposite side of the dog from the judge. When the judge is finished, you may either have your dog resume his show pose or you may relax while the judge inspects the remaining dogs.

Sometimes, even after weeks of training and preparation, you may freeze and suddenly forget how to handle your dog. If this happens, simply watch an experienced handler and imitate him. Keep in mind that judging a class of dogs usually doesn't take very long and you'll be out of the ring before you know it.

If your dog wins a ribbon, no matter what color, be sure to thank the judge graciously. If your dog did not win first place, extend your sincere congratulations to the winner.

What do Judges look for in the show ring?

A good judge begins immediately sorting out the quality dogs as they go around the ring. These are the dogs with heads up and tails moving, dogs who are enjoying themselves. While the dogs are making their first laps around the ring, judges quickly appraise the top lines, gaits, personalities, and overall appearances. Later, during the inspection of individual dogs, a judge assesses the fine points of conformation: head, bite, shoulder, drape of stifle, and so forth.

Most judges try to look at the total dog, rather than get distracted by a specific part. They don't award points to each separate part of the dog, rather, it's how the various components fit together that counts; a great head is valueless on a cow-hocked specimen.

Judging dogs is far from an exact science. "Symmetry," "balance," "contour," "profile," "gait," and "expression" are all inexact principles, yet they comprise the foundation of judging dogs. To apply these principles, one must have an eye for a dog. Most judges have developed this ability after years of exhibiting, breeding, handling, and judging dogs; therefore, their impressions are based on their unique experiences as well as on instinct and aesthetic values.

An exhibitor can do himself a very big favor by knowing his dog's strong and weak points. He wouldn't want to push a poor head at the judge, but might want to pull the dog's ears over his head to show his beautiful shoulders.

Dog gaiting enjoying self

Judges are impressed with good muscle tone and clean dogs. This means that ears and mouth, as well as coat, should be clean.

Sometimes exhibitors seem bent on self-destruction. They try so hard to cover up faults and end up achieving just the opposite. Any handler who keeps rearranging the dog's front is going to pique the judge's curiosity and who knows what he may find. Don't overhandle your dog. Stay in the background, and don't "showboat." The judge is interested in the dog, not you.

Judges do not like excessive baiting. It often gives an artificial impression and creates slobbering jaws. Keep it to a minimum and use it primarily to get the dog's head in the right position and then hold it still.

There are many reasons – some obvious, others subtle – why different judges would select different winners from the same class of dog. The most apparent reason is that some judges simply prefer one

Why might different judges select different winners from the same class of dogs?

type over another. For example, one judge may prefer a utilitarian, sporting look in an English Cocker Spaniel, while another may consider beauty to be the most important feature.

The mood and appearance of a dog on a particular day also affects the judge's decision. In fact, sometimes the same judge, judging the same dogs,

Lining up dogs for inspection

may select different winners on different days. Yes, this can be confusing and upsetting to exhibitors. Try to keep in mind, though, that dogs have off days just like people. Some days they may be reluctant to really step around a show ring. Also, some dogs just do better at an outdoor show than at an indoor show, or vice versa.

Beyond these somewhat obvious factors, though, lies the psychological makeup of the individual judge. People who are basically indecisive in their personal makeup will also tend to be indecisive judges. They may know their breeds but will have a difficult time making judgments and final decisions. Others may be forceful and dominant, easily selecting the winners from each class, but they may also tend to be inflexible and unwilling to learn. Then, too, you may encounter judges who are so poorly organized they have no control of the ring, and the resulting chaos fosters poor presentations by both handlers and dogs.

In short, a judge's psychological makeup carries over into the ring and affects all participants, handlers and dogs alike. Unfortunately, there is no way to prepare for the assorted personalities you will face in the ring. Try to remain flexible and remember the judge is also human, has feelings as well as off days, and also has a life outside the show ring.

If you genuinely feel that a judge is unfair, you can discuss your concerns with the AKC field representative at the show. Check at the show superintendent's desk, which is generally located at a central place at each show, for the whereabouts of the AKC field representative.

You can better your dog's chances of winning by keeping notes on the judges he faces. (An interesting aside: 15 percent of the judges perform 85 percent of the judging; so, learning about their preferences is easier than it appears.) Some judges are more likely than others to select your dog as a winner. This is because different judges tend to place varying importance on different aspects of a dog. For example, one judge may consider a good head to be the most important single feature of your breed, while another may look most favorably on dogs with good movement. By keeping detailed records of how your dog places under different judges, you will be able to select which judges to show your dog under. You can, in this way, actually improve your dog's chances of winning.

Can I improve my dog's chances of winning?

However, winning in this manner also has its drawbacks. You may face nagging doubts about whether your dog can beat all comers under any conditions. You may question your own motives: Are you trying simply to accumulate points on your dog or are you competing honorably for the betterment of the breed? Everyone knows that it's more fun to win than lose. When your dog can win under any conditions, against any competitors, is the most satisfying feeling of all.

How does a good sport behave at shows?

With the odds of winning at only about 60 percent – even for a very good dog – you will enjoy the sport more if you know how to lose graciously. This may seem as though it would not be too difficult, but you may be amazed at how much of one's ego is riding on the judge's decision. If you can, extend your genuine congratulations to the winners. By doing so, you will generate good feelings on many different levels: within yourself, between you and the winner, and within the dog show community as a whole.

When your dog wins in the ring, you will be thrilled. You will probably want to share your joy with everyone, but you can't just yet. Why not? Because the people and dogs nearest to you at the moment of victory are the same ones you just beat in the ring. Politely accept any congratulations, but try to contain your elation until a more appropriate moment.

What does it take to be a good winner?

Let's say you have followed all the foregoing good advice. You have set out on your own and fortune has smiled upon you. Everything is wonderful. You are a winner and you bask in the reflected glory of your winning dogs. Great, except that with all your

A good winner

winning, things are not quite right. You have the uncomfortable feeling that all your winning is not going over too well with your fellow exhibitors. Where did you go wrong? Let's look into this part of the sport a bit more.

Much emphasis has been placed on being a good sport and taking your losses in stride. This shouldn't be so hard because most of us lose more than we win. We have lots of experience with losing. But now the tables are turned – you are a consistent winner. Acting appropriately as a winner is something else indeed.

At any show, whether it is a Specialty or an All-Breed, there can only be a few winners in each breed. If one exhibitor's entries account for more than one win, the possibilities become even smaller. This means only a small number of people go home perfectly happy. The vast majority console themselves that there will be another day or that at least the judge did a conscientious job and gave them a fair shake.

You will learn that it is hard to be a winner. Although your goal is to be a winner and to get to the top, sometimes that winning spirit can get you into trouble with your peers. Because of that, reaching the summit can seem a hollow triumph. Your dog has won, you're thrilled, elated, on cloud nine and you want to shout about it from the roof tops and let the world know about your accomplishments. But you don't, or you learn to use other avenues. Let's face it, you're happy, but most of the other exhibitors are not. So it's best to adopt the reserve of the British and smile inwardly.

So you see being a winner is not easy no matter how desirable the purple ribbon looks from afar. Take care.

CHAPTER SUMMARY:

A dog must be registered with the AKC before it can be shown.

Pack your car the night before the show; remember to take along the entry packet mailed to you by the show superintendent.

To impress a judge, make sure your dog is well groomed for the show, arrive at the ring on time, and handle the dog with confidence.

Your dog will probably not win every time, even if he is of high quality. Nonetheless, enter the ring expecting to win.

While in the ring, always keep your dog between you and the judge.

Most judges are impressed with the overall appearance of a dog, rather than just one of its individual parts.

The results of judging may vary depending on the judges's "type" preference, the mood of the dog on the day of the show, and the psychological makeup of the individual judge.

You can improve your dog's chances of winning if you show only under judges who like your "type" of dog. However, playing the odds like this may leave you unsure of your dog's ability to win under less ideal circumstances.

When your dog wins, display your joy with restraint and accept congratulations politely. When your dog loses, congratulate the winner.

Fifteen percent of the judges judge 85 percent of the shows.

6 Every Dog Has His Day

"or, you can't win
every time"

As John Wayne would say, "Let's get this straight right now," your dog is not going to win at every show, nor is he going to perform the same at every show. Dogs have their days.

I once had the good fortune to be judging a Futurity and was blessed by the presence of an outstanding puppy. I was quite taken with this young dog and gave him the top award. He went on to go Best of Winners at that same show. He launched his Specials career in the same spectacular manner.

Later that year, I was in his part of the country and looking forward to judging this excellent specimen again. In came the Specials class. There was his handler, but who was that dog at the other end of the lead? This dog looked "hang-dog," his coat had no luster and he showed poorly. Needless to say, he got passed by that day. However, three months later at a show some distance from his home base, I once again judged him. On this occasion, he came into the ring like he was answering a three-alarm fire – beautiful coat showing all the highlights, head up and proud. Here was the same dog and the same judge, but different circumstances. AG

As one new to the dog show game, you need to appreciate that dogs are under a great deal of stress. It is an intense experience for them and they burn a lot of calories during a show. Being confined to a crate most of the day, riding from one strange place

How do dogs react to the rigors of the dog show game?

to another, and being separated from their owners are very hard on dogs.

Because they can't speak out and tell you their problems, you need to observe their behavior and performances. An article in *The Oregonian* on pet stress points out that "recent technical advances reveal that pets can face the same health risks as people, such as hypertension." You and your dog share the same risks that stress presents.

Some dogs handle all this with aplomb. Others react with varying symptoms, often failing to respond to their handlers' wishes. I know many a handler who has come out of the ring cursing the handful he had to contend with that go-around.

Most animals are happiest when they have a standard routine. They get let out to their runs at a certain time; they get fed at a certain time, and in the same place. Kennel or home surroundings are constant. They gain confidence by this routine. They know what and when to expect things to happen. In effect, they are in control. Now, you take that same well-adjusted dog to a handler. First off, he is in a strange environment. He is not sure where he is supposed to go or what he supposed to do. His feeding schedule and often his food are different. He enters into a training program that is foreign to him. He eventually gains confidence in his handler, but things are not the same.

Just as he gets used to this routine, he is tucked into a crate, put in some kind of vehicle, and driven many miles away. He gets hauled out into unfamiliar surroundings again and has to perform in a strange setting. (Happily, most of the time he can do it.) Then, once again, he's tucked into his crate and is off to another show on the circuit. The handler can't pay much attention to him because he has a full slate of dogs entered. So, the dog gets a quick brush out, a cluck under the chin and he's expected to do his thing to perfection.

Is it any wonder that sometimes these great dogs "go off their feed?" They can handle only so much stress and then there is a breaking point. This point, like the one for humans, differs with the individual dog. He may react in a number of ways: hanging back on the lead, not wanting to enter the ring, or not responding at all to the handler.

In addition to these psychological reactions, a dog may exhibit physical symptoms that can include: a dull coat, although he may be eating well; pulling back on the lead as though he were suffering from tonsillitis, but the vet doesn't see any inflammation; whimpering when touched in certain places, but there's no evidence of bruises or wounds. These symptoms are reactions to situations a dog cannot handle. He wants to withdraw and unconsciously chooses the route that works best for him.

Dogs do become really ill while being shown, but that is another matter and can be dealt with by a vet.

To the stress that the dog is experiencing, add the handler's disposition and mental and physical health, and you can begin to understand why odd things can happen on any given day.

How can I insure that my dogs will win more regularly and be able to handle the stress?

Let's start by acknowledging that good temperament is essential in any breed. This means that the dog has to come from parents and grandparents who exhibited these qualities. Today, a big thing is made of behavioral testing to see which puppies in a litter can react to strange and challenging situations and not panic or attack.

There has grown up a whole body of literature on this very subject. Probably one of the best books to read is Clarence Pfaffenberger's *New Knowledge of Dog Behavior* (Howell Book House), which is about choosing guide dogs for the blind. Another resource is a series of articles written in 1990 by Dr. Ian Dunbar for the *AKC Gazette*. In one article, he points out:

"The quality of a dog's behavior, temperament and training varies inversely with the number of dogs in the household. Most dog fanciers start with a single dog which is both a pet and a show dog. Additional dogs are acquired along the way and, at some point, many breeders opt for outdoor kennels to accommodate their growing dog population.

"Kennel dogs receive less human attention and affection than household pets. Most breeders are women, and less than 40 percent of breeders have

Encourage him in new situations

children living at home. This means many puppies and adult dogs sold as pets have seldom met children or men (the two most common stimuli for fearfulness and aggression), are seldom exposed to the confusing commotion and cacophony of an ever changing domestic environment and are less likely to be walked regularly, where they would meet a wide variety of human strangers as well as other dogs and animals in differing urban and rural settings."

It is easy to see that the dog you purchased as your show dog may have come from just such an environment. Not that he hasn't been raised well and shows some equilibrium, but he may not be ready or able to handle the new world you have thrust him into.

While a dog's basic personality is set at an early age, you still can help your dog and yourself by building on the foundation you have. Take your dog with you on walks. Take him to the mall (if he's allowed there), take him to outdoor shopping centers, and take him on short rides while in his crate that don't end up at the vet's or the boarding kennel.

Reassure him at all times when he comes across a strange situation and is not sure how to react. Be positive and don't drag him into frightening situations telling him he's a crybaby and should be bold and aggressive. Buddy, if you do that I can guarantee a problem dog.

Go with your handler to the dog's first shows. Let him know that you are there and pet him a lot. Slowly, he will make the transfer to his handler and you'll probably become jealous because the dog seems to prefer this other person to you.

Keep you expectations reasonable. If this is your first dog, the breeder probably didn't sell you a Best in Show specimen. You may more likely have a finishable dog. Having him finish his championship is surely better than a sharp stick in the eye, so show him, enjoy him, and most of all, love him.

CHAPTER SUMMARY:

Dogs are susceptible to health risks produced by stress.

Most dogs are happiest when they have a standard routine.

Dogs react to stress by exhibiting both physical and psychological symptoms.

Try to buy a dog whose parents and grandparents had even temperaments.

Build a strong foundation of trust between you and your dog.

Keep your expectations reasonable.

Selecting a Handler

Many people in this wacky sport of purebred dogs have a prejudiced view of the professional handler, especially neophyte exhibitors. They see the handlers garner the majority of top wins and hear the ringside chatter that the handlers have an "in" with the judges and that the fix is on and only the handlers will win that day. Poppycock!

Many neophytes can't handle their way out of a paper bag. They make their dogs look so bad they couldn't win if they were showing Rin Tin Tin incarnate.

As these neophytes progress, so do their skills, but, by and large, they don't stack up in trimming, training and conditioning with expert professional handlers. You will note that I said expert. Handlers come in various gradations of skill just like actors, lawyers, etc.

Many moons ago, the AKC licensed handlers and its requirements were tough. Basically, would-be handlers had to serve apprenticeships under other handlers, have adequate kennel facilities, be recommended by their mentors, and be fiscally responsible. Then, and only then, would they be granted licenses and be allowed to call themselves professional handlers.

Since the AKC dropped its oversight of handlers, anyone may call himself an agent or handler. So beware and follow the old rule of the marketplace – *caveat emptor.*

There are two major associations attempting to bring professionalism back to the ranks of handlers.

The oldest is the Professional Handlers Association (PHA), which existed prior to AKC's withdrawal. The other is the Handlers Guild. Membership in these groups indicates adherence to their guidelines and code of ethics.

Most new exhibitors start by showing their own dogs. When they become discouraged with their lack of winning, they turn to handlers, and if the handlers are successful with their dogs, never venture into the showring again except at matches.

Well, my friend, if this is your plan, you've got the cart before the horse. Recognize that you probably are not going to look like one of the world's greatest handlers in the ring at first – don't expect to! In fact, you may be better off to put your dog with an expert handler and observe how he shows and trims your dog. Watch carefully how the dog is posed, gaited and prepared for the ring. Pay for your lessons early in the game from the best and then try your wings.

You will find that with a role model your performance will dramatically improve. You will learn what the judge looks for, how to behave in the ring and how to stack and gait your dog properly. It may well be your salvation as an amateur handler, and by learning to compete with the best of them you can WIN on your own.

For greater insights into what can go wrong in the ring, send for the AKC's delightful video, *A Day in the Ring with Mr. Wrong*. For information on all dog-related videos and AKC breed standard videos, see *The Canine Source Book* (Susan Bulanda, Doral Publishing, Inc., 1990). AG

When does a dog need a professional handler?

If your dog consistently wins or places high in the best of breed competition, you could have a top-winning show dog on your hands. However, to achieve his potential, your dog must be shown to his full advantage – and this is something you are probably not experienced enough to do yet. This is the reason why most top-winning show dogs are shown by professional handlers, and not by their owners. However, once you gain experience showing, it is possible that you could show and compete with the best.

The best way to search for a handler is to study dog magazines and newspapers, such as *Kennel Review*, *Dog Fancy*, *Dog News*, *Dog World*, and *The Canine Chronicle*, as well as your breed magazines, taking note of those handlers who live in your area and who handle your breed of dog. Also, you should contact one of the associations and ask for a list of local

How can I find a handler for my dog?

Professional dog handlers earn their living by showing dogs. Aspiring owners of top-quality dogs contract with handlers to board, groom, care for, train, and exhibit their dogs.

What is a professional handler, and where does he get his training?

Most handlers start out as dog breeders and spend years learning the ins and outs of the dog show game before becoming professional handlers. At first, they will usually only handle the breed of dog they know best before branching out to handle other breeds. For example, if Joe Smith spent 10 years breeding and exhibiting Poodles, he would probably begin his professional handling career by showing other people's Poodles. Next, he might choose to branch out to other dogs in the Non-Sporting Group, and then to the other groups. Be aware, though, that not all handlers show all types of dogs. Some of the top handlers in the country handle dogs from just one group.

Although most handlers start out as breeders, some begin as handlers' apprentices or assistants. Apprentices help the handler with all aspects of dog handling: kennel care, grooming, shuttling dogs to and from the show ring, and, sometimes, with exhibiting. After serving in this capacity for a number of years, an assistant can strike out on his own, fully trained and experienced. The apprenticeship system seems to work well; many top-notch handlers throughout the country have started this way.

Most handlers belong to the Professional Handlers' Association (PHA) or the Handlers Guild. These business organizations endeavor to improve the business practices of their members, maintain a code of ethics, and serve as a source of referrals and information for handlers and for dog owners. You can usually recognize PHA or Guild members at dog shows by the pins on their lapels.

handlers. After developing a list of several qualified handlers, attend one or two shows and watch them at work. Look for handlers who present themselves well, who treat their dogs with respect and affection, and who graciously accept the judge's decision. Then, contact the ones who most impress you to discuss their qualifications, availability and rates.

Be aware, though, that a top-quality professional handler will only accept a dog that has a good chance of finishing his championship. To do otherwise would serve to downgrade the handler's professional reputation, and would also be a waste of the dog owner's money.

What qualities should I look for in a handler?

When meeting with a prospective handler for your dog, look for several key qualities:

1. Professionalism. Choose a handler who looks and acts professional. Scrutinize the handler's personal grooming habits; you cannot reasonably expect a handler to groom your dog properly if his own grooming habits are deficient.
2. Strong sense of ethics. Select a handler who is ethical and whose business practices are sound. Ask for a rate card, current references, and, if you decide to hire the handler, a written contract. A handler with a strong standard of ethics will be pleased to provide you with this basic, and important, information.
3. Competitive nature. Look for a handler who exhibits a competitive, honest nature. Yes, it's great to win all the time, but make sure the handler wins fair and square. Remember, while in the show ring, your handler represents you.
4. Experience. Select a handler who has experience showing your type of dog.

Will the handler take my dog full time?

Handlers generally prefer to accept dogs on a full-time, live-in basis for the following reasons:
- The handler can get to know the dog's personality and moods. By doing so, the handler will be able to base his handling techniques on the needs of the dog.
- The dog will be used to the handler, and, therefore, will usually respond better in the ring.

Professionalism

- The handler can exercise the dog and train him for the show ring.
- The handler can bathe and groom the dog properly before each show.

Although a handler generally prefers to take a dog on a full-time basis, sometimes he will agree to show your dog as a "ringside pick-up." In other words, the handler will meet you and your dog at the show, and will groom and show your dog that day.

The ringside pick-up arrangement can be beneficial to both handler and owner under certain conditions. For example, the handler may not have room for your dog if he already has a full load of live-in dogs. Thus, a part-time arrangement may be the only way for this particular handler to show your dog.

Additionally, for the dog's owner, ringside pick-up is much less costly than a full-time arrangement. On the other hand, the handler may not be able to show your dog if there is a conflict with the schedule of full-time dogs.

How do handlers set their rates? Handlers generally charge a flat rate to train, groom, and show a dog. This flat rate typically includes the show entry fees and transportation to and from shows. In addition to this flat rate, there can be many extra charges, including:
- board, which is usually based on the size of the dog;
- any necessary veterinary assistance;
- a bonus for winning or placing your dog in Group or Best in Show competitions.

Fig. 3. Professional Handler's rate card. Courtesy of Robert and Delores Burkholder

RATES

Handling Fee Per Show $55.00

Coated and Large Breeds 65.00

Specialty Shows 75.00

Board Per Day. 5.00

ADDITIONAL CHARGES

Best In Show 200.00

Group 1 . . . . 50.00

2 . . . . 40.00

3 . . . . 30.00

4 . . . . 20.00

Prestige Shows & National Specialities . . . Fees On Request

Airport Pickup or Delivery 25.00

Retainer In Advance 300.00

POLICY

Bills due upon receipt — Interest charges at rate of 1.5% on unpaid balances after 30 days — Ribbons, tear sheets and trophies will be sent as soon as possible after each show — Cash awards will be retained by the handler — All phone calls will be collect — In case of ring conflicts, I will use my judgment and either pull the dog or find another competent handler for the dog — Dogs must be current on shots and free of parasites — Handling fees will be charged unless entry is cancelled before closing date.

Most professional handlers will provide you with a rate card and a contract for services. You might want to take the contract home and study it, along with the rate card, before making a decision.

Note the following important points:

- Any additional compensation based on higher awards
- First-call charges
- When handler may decline to continue handling dog

Will the handler ask me to sign a contract for services?

Given the expense involved, you might want to develop a plan to help you better afford the services of a professional handler. For example, you could wait until your dog is 15 months old before showing it. This would give the dog time to mature, and would also allow you to save money for the dog's show career. Next, you could ask your handler to show your dog as a ringside pick-up until the dog's championship is finished. Then, if your dog finishes his championship easily, and if you want to further pursue the dog's show career, you may turn your dog over to the handler for six months on a full-time basis. At the end of that time, you should re-evaluate your dog's potential career as well as the ambitions you hold for your dog.

How can I minimize the expense of a professional handler?

CHAPTER SUMMARY:

If your dog consistently places high in its variety or breed, you may want to consider the services of a professional dog handler.

Most handlers start out as breeders or as handlers' apprentices.

Look for the following qualities when selecting a handler for your dog: professionalism, a strong sense of ethics, a competitive nature, and experience with your breed of dog.

Handlers show dogs on both a full-time live-in basis, as well as on a part-time ringside pick-up basis.

Study the handler's rate card and contract before making a commitment.

8

Campaigning a Top Winner

"migraine alley"

Yes, you may reach this pinnacle of success. You're reading this book because you're not there yet and want desperately to "arrive."

There are a variety of paths to take to reach this lofty goal. You can unlimber your checkbook and try to buy a top-rated dog with an ready-made reputation (do check with your handler or a serious breeder before doing this). You can continue with this dog's handler and bask in the glory of owning a top one.

Buy best in show dog

Another, perhaps less expensive way, is to become a co-owner. You will be expected to foot most of the handling bills and probably won't have much to say about the dog's career or future breeding. However, you will be part of a winning team, and if the social whirl is your thing, these first two paths can get you invited to the right parties.

Path number three is to buy a dog being campaigned to his championship, but not yet there. The dog will be trained, conditioned and ready, and you'll be able to make all the decisions regarding his future. (Again, before doing this, seek advice so you don't make a costly mistake.)

Path number four, employed by most people, is the purchase of a young and promising specimen. It's usually the least expensive way initially, but training and conditioning are your responsibilities. Whether the dog ever reaches the exalted ranks of championship status depends both on how he develops as a dog and how you develop as a trainer and exhibitor.

It's important to note that not every champion is a Specials dog. This is a lofty plateau with tough competition. Perhaps only one in ten champions belongs in this distinguished group. Only about 1.2 percent of the dogs of your breed ever reach the Best in Group or Best in Show level. Another 3 percent achieve Best of Variety or Best of Breed winners. This leaves a lot of dogs on the outside looking in. AG

What is a Specials dog, and what are the benefits of owning one?

If your dog earned his championship in short order, and appears to have the potential to win his breed again and again, you may decide to campaign him as a Specials dog. Seriously campaigning a dog is costly, requiring about $25,000 a year to cover handler's fees, travel to distant shows, advertising and promotion expenses. Only a small portion of this expense may be recouped in stud fees if your dog is a male.

In addition to the financial cost, campaigning a Specials dog expends an abundance of emotional energy. For example, if you choose not to travel to all the dog shows, you may end up with frazzled nerves waiting for that phone call from your handler reporting the results of the most recent competition.

Young, promising specimen

But the emotional payback is well worth it, just ask the enthusiastic owner of any top-winning dog. You can look forward to many thrilling weekends, and your shelves may soon be filled with gleaming trophies.

When you campaign a dog, like it or not, you automatically enter another contest outside the show ring: the contest for show-win points. A number of dog publications keep track of dogs' accumulated wins and rank the winning dogs by breed, group, and all-breed. These publications usually publish their statistics quarterly. Once your dog reaches the big time, you can become consumed with a passion to have it ranked in the top 10.

How do I campaign a Specials dog?

Start by showing your dog under judges who have previously awarded your dog a Best of Breed or Variety. Next, show under judges with sound reputations – judges who will give your dog a fair shake. Even after your dog's show career is established, however, don't enter every show; judges differ in their ability to judge. Work with your handler to prepare a list of competent judges under whom you will show your dog and who like your type of dog.

Then, advertise your dog's winnings in well-established specialty and all-breed dog magazines and newspapers. This will make the dog better known and could enhance his chances of winning. Also, if your dog is a male, advertising can bring in larger and more frequent stud fees.

Last, know when to quit. Set goals that can be achieved realistically and stick with them. For example, if 50 Best of Breed wins within two years is your goal, quit when you get there. Also, in order to maintain good relations with other breeders, let your goals be known. Your fellow competitors will likely be unhappy when you capture all the wins, but they can survive and maintain hope for their own goals, if they know there will be an end to your reign. When deciding how long to show your dog, consider that most people campaign their Specials dogs for only two or three years.

How do I advertise a Specials dog?

Advertising your dog is an art in itself. The best way to go about it is to run continual ads in the breed and all-breed magazines. Show recent, excellent-quality photographs of your dog, varying the shots from posed show wins to informal shots. At first, the ad's text should stress show wins. Later, the text should note the bitches being bred to your dog, especially if they are from well-known and respected

86   □   Part II. Exhibiting

Fig. 4. Example of published list of top-winning dogs Courtesy of Kennel Review Magazine

FIRST QUARTER REPORT

THRU AND INCLUDING SHOWS OF JANUARY 31, 1990, AS REPORTED IN THE *AKC AWARDS.*

TOP TWENTY TERRIER		
1.	CH. KERRAGEEN'S HOTSPUR *Kerry*	7,637
2.	CH. LOULINE HEAD OVER HEELS *Wire Fox*	6,661
3.	CH. CALKERRY EVENING ATTIRE *Welsh*	6,307
4.	CH. HUGO'S PRANCER *Norfolk*	4,100
5.	CH. HOLYROOD'S HOOTMAN OF SHELYBAY *West Highland White*	3,366
6.	CH. ROUGH N READY RECRUIT *Irish Terrier*	2,983
7.	CH. TORSET TOUCH OF CLASS *Sealyham*	2,344
8.	CH. KILLICK OF THE MESS *Wire Fox*	2,256
9.	CH. TWEED TAKE BY STORM *West Highland White*	2,221
10.	CH. BLACKDALE AUTOCRAT *Wire Fox*	2,146
11.	CH. KETKA QWIK CHARGE OF DALFOX *Border*	2,099
12.	CH. ANDOVER SONG N DANCE MAN *Soft Coated Wheaten*	2,066
13.	CH. RIGHTLY SO ORIGINAL SIN *Norfolk*	2,039
14.	CH. SAPHIRE STAR OF SILVERBUSH *Wire Fox*	1,909
15.	CH. SUNSPRYTE GREGMAR JEWEL *Welsh*	1,737
16.	CH. MCVAN'S SANDMAN *Scottish Terrier*	1,678
17.	CH. PRINCIPALS MACGYVER *West Highland White*	1,591
18.	CH. STONEBROKE FEATHER IN MY HAT *SEALYHAM*	1,320
19.	CH. ABINGTON'S WINGATE'S FANCY *Dandie Dinmont*	1,190
20.	CH. WILLOW WIND CENTURIAN *Bedlington*	1,163

TOP TWENTY NON SPORTING		
1.	CH. WHISPERWIND'S ON A CAROUSEL *Standard Poodle*	16,310
2.	CH. DASSIN MARJARITA *Standard Poodle*	6,820
3.	CH. TED-EL HALO JET SETTER *Standard Poodle*	5,777
4.	CH. HETHERBULL BOUNTY'S FRIGATE *Bulldog*	4,324
5.	CH. HETHERBULL ARROGANT RONALD *Bulldog*	4,315
6.	CH. RUFKINS CHIP OFF THE OL ROCK *Lhasa Apso*	4,011
7.	CH. RICKSHAW EPIC BILLY B *Chow Chow*	3,067
8.	CH. CHAMINADE LE BLANC CHAMOUR *Bichon Frise*	3,065
9.	CH. VANDYS MALIK *Keeshond*	2,836
10.	CH. RENJO'S FAST EDDIE *Miniature Poodle*	2,590
11.	CH. PLAYER EDWARDPUCK *French Bulldog*	2,358
12.	CH. BARKINGS SHIMMER OF WILDWAYS *Miniature Poodle*	1,537
13.	CH. BO-DEN CEDARCREST PRIVATE EYE *Keeshond*	1,489
14.	CH. SEA STAR'S CASANOVA *Bichon Frise*	1,440
15.	CH. WYNWOOD'S FUZZBUSTER *Lhasa Apso*	1,367
16.	CH. ST FLORIAN PISCES JORDACHE *Dalmatian*	1,362
17.	CH. KARELEA BAR KING BUTTERFLY *Miniature Poodle*	1,349
18.	CH. GORGIS BLUE SKIES ALICE B *Standard Poodle*	1,340
19.	CH. D'BARA DESIREE *Standard Poodle*	1,339
20.	CH. BONDSAI'S BULLET HITTH BULLSI *Chow Chow*	1,235

TOP TWENTY TOY		
1.	CH. TREYACRES ZORRO *Brussels Griffon*	8,007
2.	CH. SAND ISLAND SMALL KRAFT LITE *Maltese*	7,466
3.	CH. WENDESSA CROWN PRINCE *Pekingese*	5,626
4.	CH. ROWELL'S SOLO MOON RISING *Pug*	4,569
5.	CH. CAMELOT ALLIAGE *Toy Poodle*	4,563
6.	CH. SNOBHILL'S FREE LANCE *Shih Tzu*	3,583
7.	CH. CAMEOS COVER GIRL *Pug*	3,344
8.	CH. SUNBROOK BUCKSKIN GAL *Miniature Pinscher*	3,105
9.	CH. BIENAIMEE MINO MAYO MINO-BEE	2,935
10.	CH. JO-LI WIND IN THE WILLOWS *Pekingese*	2,922
11.	CH. TREBOR OF AHS BRAND *Toy Poodle*	2,670
12.	CH. WYCHMIRAMAR-SWEET BABY JAMES *Shih Tzu*	2,558
13.	CH. SU-DAWN'S PEE WEE HERMAN *Affenpinscher*	2,268
14.	CH. SALUTAIRE UNFORGETTABLE *Toy Manchester*	2,041
15.	CH. HOMESTEADS BOSS OF TREYACRES *Brussels Griffon*	1,736
16.	CH. JODAN'S WINTER DESTINY *Toy Poodle*	1,685
17.	CH. ELADREWS EXQUISITE *Chihuahua-Long*	1,631
18.	CH. DARRETTE'S RIVALLRY *Toy Poodle*	1,535
19.	CH. JAMOL'S KLASSIC HI TIME *Pomeranian*	1,490
20.	CH. DESMOND'S MERRY MAKER *Chihuahua-Smooth*	1,489

TOP TWENTY HERDING		
1.	CH. GALBRAITH'S IRONEYES *Bouvier Des Flandres*	16,972
2.	CH. QUICHES IVANHOE *Bouvier Des Flandres*	10,176
3.	CH. GALEWYND'S GEORGIO ARMANI *German Shepherd Dog*	6,394
4.	CH. MASQUERADE PAR-T-AT SU GRAN *Old English Sheepdog*	3,108
5.	CH. MARWAL STEPPIN' OUT *Shetland Sheepdog*	3,077
6.	CH. CARETTI'S AUTOBAHN *German Shepherd Dog*	2,933
7.	CH. SHADOW HILL'S JAZZ ON PRINHILL *Shetland Sheepdog*	2,887
8.	CH. SOLOWAY GRAND COUP *Bouvier Des Flandres*	2,592
9.	CH. STONEHAVEN'S PRIMROSE LANE C.D. *Shetland Sheepdog*	2,025
10.	CH. MERIT'S RAYS OF SUNSHINE *Rough Collie*	1,972
11.	CH. FOXBRIDES MCLAUGHLAN *Smooth Collie*	1,478
12.	CH. ROUGHOUSE PENNINGTON DARYL *Pembroke Welsh Corgi*	1,464
13.	CH. RENEFIELD ROCKHOPPER *Pembroke Welsh Corgi*	1,442
14.	CH. MOONSHADOW'S PUTTIN ON THE RITZ *Puli*	1,356
15.	CH. WALLBANGER XTRATERRESTRIAL *Puli*	1,330
16.	CH. BRITANNIA SWEET LADY C.D. *Bearded Collie*	1,277
17.	CH. INCANDESENT LIMITED EDITION *Rough Collie*	1,163
18.	CH. DONAMIK'S CRUSADING RAIDER C.D. *Bouvier Des Flandres*	1,141
19.	CH. SOUVENIRS TRIPLE PLAY *Belgian Tervuren*	1,140
20.	CH. FOX MEADOWS OBSESSION *Pembroke Welsh Corgi*	1,105

Fig. 5. Example of ad promoting Specialty winner

..."Beemer"

Twice winner of the National Specialty.
Number One Non Sporting Dog on the West
Coast 1990 / Group First Westminster K.C.

Owners:
Mrs. William Morrow and
Richard & Carolyn Vida

blood lines, and, finally, wins of the dog's offspring. Be sure to emphasize group and all-breed wins.

Another form of positive advertising is to send a good picture of each Group and Best in Show win to each judge, thanking him for awarding the win to your dog. (Almost all dog shows are attended by professional dog-show photographers who send photographs to the exhibitor for review and purchase.) The picture should show the dog being awarded the ribbon by the judge. Remember, though, it must also be a good picture of the judge.

What is a first-call dog?

Often the handler you choose has other dogs of top rank. In breeds that are divided by color or coat, he may have two other dogs of that breed, or he may have top winners in your group or in other groups.

This can pose a real dilemma. Which dog receives priority, or "first-call" status? Sometimes it's based on the seniority of the dogs in his string or the seniority of the clients. If all are equal, the client willing to pay for first call has his dog given priority.

More often than not, you as a new client will have to learn to live with the fact that your dog may be shown by the handler's assistant, or he may engage another top-flight handler in return for reciprocal services.

It's there and it's a fact of life. Learn to live with it until you become more senior in the ranks.

CHAPTER SUMMARY:

Campaigning a Specials dog is an expensive and emotional roller coaster ride, but most owners of top-winning show dogs agree that it's worth the expense.

Plan your dog's show career: Under which judges will you show? How will you advertise your dog? How many wins or how many years will you campaign your dog before retiring him?

Understand the concept of first call and how to adapt to the practice.

9

How to Advertise What You've Got

"come blow your horn"

Once you've gotten your feet wet in this game you begin to crave some recognition for your efforts. You read the breed magazine and see all the ads and think, hey, why not me?

In the beginning, you might as well save your money. Advertising a non-product is money down the drain. Many small kennels and beginning breeders do take a one-inch ad in the breed magazine on a yearly contract basis to get their names before the public. It also helps get a larger discount when you do have something later to crow about.

By and large though, it does not pay off other than in ego satisfaction to see your newly minted kennel name in print. However, if it makes you happy, do it! The magazine publishers will appreciate your business. The real payoff comes later when you have steak to sell, not just the sizzle.

More money is wasted on poor advertising than on feeding your dogs. In America, we have created a wonderful fallacy that advertising can sell anything. Madison Avenue thrives on this approach. It is just not true. Proper, planned advertising can pay off if you have the right product at the right time and know how to merchandise it.

Just because you have what you think is a great son of Ch. Sunny Jim, and with his pedigree he should be a great producer, don't think the world will beat a path to your door if you mention this fact in a print ad. What if another Sunny Jim son (after all he is a top producer) is dusting off all comers in the show ring and his progeny are already hitting the show ring. What if his owners are spending big bucks advertising this fact? Where does this leave you?

Read on and learn some of the basics of what to do and not to do when it comes to blowing your horn and promoting your dogs and your kennel. And, incidentally, if you follow this advice, how you can make your advertising investment pay off. AG

How effective is advertising?

One of the first things you should learn is that promoting a successful dog's campaign will cost almost as much in promotion costs as handling fees. No, this doesn't mean TV spots, just plain print advertising.

Most of the books on advertising caution about the often-misleading information given to prospective advertisers about the effectiveness of advertising. (See Alec Benn's book, *The 27 Most Common Mistakes in Advertising*, American Management Assoc., 1978.) Seldom are you told about the many costly campaigns that brought few, if any, stud services or sold no puppies. Only the positive is accentuated. Most people probably would spend less on advertising if they knew the odds against a successful outcome.

Much of advertising's greatest impact is on the advertisers who get big ego boosts out of seeing their ads in print, even though results are negligible. It's great to show the ad to your co-workers and to imagine the look of chagrin on the faces of your competitors.

This will be hard to swallow, but most advertising fails! If you don't believe this statement, just pick up this morning's newspaper. Look through it carefully page by page, examining each ad. Now, how many of the ads that were meant to influence you had no effect? Not even did you not read them, you probably didn't even notice them.

You can make the test with any large-circulation dog magazine you have already read. Your experience will corroborate known research in this field. On an average, the number of ads people pay some attention to during the course of a day is 76. The number they are exposed to is much higher, and 76 is simply the number a person noticed. With this kind of competition for people's minds, it is impossible for any but comparatively few ads to be effective.

Advertising research shows that few people read all the copy in an advertisement. You might wonder how many prospective dog magazine and newspaper advertisers realize that only a small percentage of the readers of any publication in which their ads appear will finish reading it. And only a small percentage of that group will be favorably influenced. If you want your ad to work well, you need to practice writing as journalists do.

The first two paragraphs of your ad should contain the well-known journalistic maxim. Give them who, what, when, why and how. When news editors need to cut stories short they can leave the first two paragraphs and the reader still gets the essence of the message.

Each succeeding piece of information expands upon what you have already told them. For example: "Ch. Whosis wins his 25th Best in Show by beating 2750 dogs at the Westminster Kennel Club's 100th Anniversary Show."

Use words properly. James J. Kilpatrick, the noted columnist, recently wrote in his syndicated column that "Mark Twain is authority for the self-evident proposition that a writer should seek the exact word and not its second cousin." Some people who write dog advertisements seem to be looking for grandfathers. Let's examine a few horrid examples:

1. A Labrador breeder seeking to impress his betters in the breed noted in his ad that his dog *suppressed* all that had come before him. Now, that's a real squelch. We know that he really meant to say surpassed.

2. A Cocker Spaniel owner who was mightily campaigning his Specials dog pointed out that his pride and joy had reached a *millennium*. This is possible, we suppose, for Webster's dictionary does give one definition as "a period of great happiness or human perfection." However, it seems a good bet he meant milestone.

3. A Poodle exhibitor seeking exalted status for his dogs pointed out that he didn't mean to cast

Fig. 6. Example of full-page ad

aspirations on his competition, but.... we think he meant aspersions.

4. Seeking a loftier plane, a Dalmatian advertiser advised owners of good bitches that by breeding to his outstanding dog they would get *famtabulous* puppies. This is one we've got to see. He probably meant to use the slang word fantabulous.

The conclusion is that if you don't know the meaning or spelling of a word, look it up. A perfectly good ad can be wrecked by such verbal gaffes.

Now that you have doubts about going ahead and advertising, let's look at some good things about print advertising and how to use it wisely. One of the axioms of advertising is: "Don't make the ad bigger than it need be." There is evidence, not widely known, that the most economical size as is the one that just dominates the page.

What factors determine the effectiveness of an ad?

A little thought shows why this is so. As the reader turns the page looking for information, the eye is most likely attracted to the largest ad on the page. Some readers may look at other ads as well, but a good number will not. The dominating ad thus gets the bonus in readership. (In publications like *Dog News*, with most of the ads occupying a full page, that effect is lost. You become just another big ad among hundreds of others.)

If the ad is any bigger than the dominating size, it attracts more readers, but not in proportion to the increase in size and cost. If the ad is just less than the dominating size, the drop in readership is likely to be disproportionately great.

There are five major categories to think about when considering what, where and how to advertise. They are:

1. How often to advertise.
2. How large the ad should be.
3. How to avoid common mistakes.
4. How to get people to do what you want them to do using words and pictures.
5. Where to place the advertising to get the best results.

How often should I advertise?

If you watch TV, you know how annoyed you get when you see a commercial over and over again. Well, that repetition turns out to be good for the advertiser – that's what makes it work. The ad won't sell unless it's shown often, and then you are more likely to remember the brand name and its favorable connotation rather than the content of the ad.

The ratio between frequency and size is not constant. This simply means that, on the average, both readership and responses increase as the size of the ad increases. However, a full-page ad will not get twice the attention of a half page. It's common sense that a half-page ad will usually be noticed by such a high percentage of readers that it would be impossible to double readership with a full page.

On the other hand, a single column ad a few inches deep might attract the attention of such a small percentage of readers that doubling its size would likely double its readership.

How big should an ad be?

How big? Nearly everyone involved in print advertising would like an ad to be larger than it should be. DON'T think big all the time. Decisions regarding the size of an ad are too often dominated by what the competition is doing rather than the principle of dominating size. The thought is that you can't go far wrong by doing what the competition is doing. But, instead of getting attention, these ads have a "me-too" look and seldom make for reader identification.

When do-as-the-competition-does is combined with even-unit-size thinking, the result is a page full of ads of the same size.

There are valid reasons, however, for making ads larger or smaller than the dominating size. It might be wise to increase the size if the subject requires the importance of a full page. Or, if the number of words is great, and/or the illustrations are large, or there are many of them. Most magazines and weekly dog newspapers have better rates for multiple insertions. You should take advantage of this bonus by taking a small one-inch yearly ad as a space holder. You can, when you have something to brag about, take advantage of the yearly rate for a sizable discount on your larger ad.

Fig. 7A. Example of same-size ads, none of which is dominant

CARALEE'S
Cocker Spaniels

Cara Napper Holland   RR 1, Box 470P12
817/444-1727   Azle, TX 76020-9456

PARTICOLOR BREEDER SINCE 1962
Joanne Thorp   13115 7½ Mile Road
414-835-1302   Caledonia, WI 53108

— watch for —
NOSOWEA'S NO PLACE LIKE HOME

BLACKS — ASCOBS
Joyce & Harry Fox   18202 Lillian Dr.
216-654-2452   Lake Milton, OH 44429

DUNDEE
C O C K E R S
CHAMPION STUD SERVICE
(All Varieties Including Browns)
Larry & Pat Vickers   Route 1, Box 296-E
601/869-7224   Saltillo, MS 38866

DENMORE'S
Dennis Messamore
Route 2, Box 68
Colfax, IL 61728
309/723-3951

**JOYARD
KENNELS**
BLACKS - B/T - BUFFS - PARTIS
Joyce Wheeler   41991 Horseshoe Rd.
813-731-3145   Punta Gorda, FL 33955

Lloyd Alton &
Bill Gorodner
(703) 777-3535

Rt. 1, Box 248C, Leesburg, VA 22075

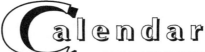

Calendar

WHEN SENDING IN SHOW DATES . . . please send in as soon as they are confirmed by the AKC and in time to be published at least once before the closing date. Be sure to include all the necessary information.

WHEN SENDING IN SHOW RESULTS . . . all show results must be received within two months after the show and must be submitted on the special forms supplied by the *Leader*. Please write or call and we'll send them to you.

The *Leader* will publish the results, write-up (optional) and win pictures at no cost to the club, except for $1.00 for return of the pictures. All show pictures must be furnished by the club. The *Leader* will not pay the photographer's charges. On the back of each picture please list the win, name of dog, sire & dam, owner, handler and the person to whom to return the picture. Be sure to include a marked catalog.

Please remember . . . show dates received too late to be published before entries close and show results received later than two months after the show will not be published.

JULY 7
Skyline Cocker Spaniel Club, Hemmens Bldg.,North & Grove Sts., Elgin, IL. Judges: Patricia Leaky, Regular Classes; and Laurabeth Duncan, Sweepstakes. Show Secretary: Prudence Gaynor, 3114 N. 77th Ave., Elmwood Park, IL 60635. Entries close June 19th.

JULY 12
Fort Vancouver Cocker Spaniel Fanciers, Inc., Hockinson Field, Brush Prairie, WA. Judges: Jeanette McGinnis, Regular Classes; Garry Fergus, Sweepstakes; and Betty Winthers, Obedience. Show Secretary: James Corbett, 20665 S.W. Johnson St., Aloha, OR 97006. Phone 503-649-2712. (Three all breed shows will follow - Greater Clark County KC, Portland KC and Willamette Valley KC, all at the same location.)

JULY 21, 22 & 23
American Spaniel Club Summer Specialty Show & Obedience Trial, Turf Valley Hotel and Country Club, Ellicott City, MD (suburb of Baltimore). Judges: Dee Dee Wood, Futurity Dog Classes, Bests of Variety & Best in Futurity; Wilma Parker, Futurity Bitch Classes; Dr. Harry Smith, Blacks; Norman Austin, Ascobs & Best of Breed; Betty Duding, Particolors, Veteran Sweepstakes & Jr. Handling; Joseph Foster, Obedience.

JULY 24
Maryland Cocker Spaniel Club, Turf Valley Hotel & Country Club, Ellicott City, MD. Judges: Norman Patton, Blacks & Best of Breed; Lewis Bayne, Ascobs, Emma Dodd, Particolors.

JULY 27
Thunder Bay Cocker Spaniel Club,
(Continued Page 64)

WILLOW VIEW
Quality & Integrity
Ascob, Parti
NANCY A.
SPINDLER
1630 Noble Rd.
Leonard, MI 48367
313/628-2926

Cashmere
Cockers
Edward & Lynn
McLoughlin
415/949-1163

2052 Jardin Dr. Mountain View, CA 94040

DEBONAIRE
Dr. & Mrs. Robert Bowman
Ashburn Plantation
Greenville, MS 38701
601/332-0533

FOX RUN FARMS
Cocker Spaniels • Ascob & Black

Carolyn Cascia
3696 Marbon Rd.
Jacksonville, FL 32223
904/268-3553

Fig. 7B. Lower right-hand ad demonstrating (1) dominance on page and (2) lack of new message

BUGLER, March 1991 — 9

Unless you include magazines when giving a forwarding address to your post office, they will destroy them. Publishers may not be notified that this is happening till 2 to 4 months later.

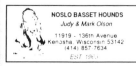
Retriever, who has just made the canine history books.

Following the immediate cheers and congratulations, there lingers a feeling of quiet respect. Smiles are exchanged and an occasional burst of celebration can be heard. The BIS winner, surrounded by ribbons and silver, poses proudly before at least a dozen cameras. Every sleepy exhibitor who remained to savor the final moments of the show is sharing the same thought, the same dream.....

As expressed so eloquently by Bill Stanfield of the *Canine Chronicle*, "Beverly Hills is about as total as a dog show can get. It's like a fine California Cabernet that gets better with each year."

(Dave Shipley, media spokesperson for US Air, confirms that no dogs were on board the ill-fated airliner that collided with a smaller comuter jet at LAX the Friday evening before this show.)

unimportant as we all glory in the quality of the dogs competing. Ch. Galbraith's Iron Eyes, the magnificent Bouvier Des Flandres, represents the Herding Group. This imposing animal took the BIS honors at this very show two years ago. Bill Cosby's Lakeland Terrier certainly has a shot at winning; in 1987 Mr. Cosby's Wire Fox Terrier, Ch. Sylair Special Edition, was Best In Show.

As Mr. Farnandeze Cartwright studies the dogs under him, each hoping for that point of the finger distinguishing them as the Best In Show winner, the enormous arena is silent. The hustle and bustle of the day seems far removed from this quiet, somber moment. Mr. Cartwright assembles the trophy presenters near the center of the ring and then that special nod goes to Ch. Vanreel Magnum of Stonecrest, a Golden

Also, when considering moving from a half-page to a full-page ad note that the rates for a full page are not always double the half-page rate.

Avoid classic common pitfalls in advertising. For example, award-winning ads are generally beautiful and entertaining, but the fact is that an ugly ad – even one that is repulsive to some readers – can be effective. Check the current ads on drug use in newspapers and on TV. Good photographs usually gain more attention than drawings or paintings and are more convincing. (Don't take this to mean you should run an airbrushed version of the perfect dog.) Readers accept photos as objective and real, ESPECIALLY if they are unretouched.

What are the pitfalls and pratfalls of advertising?

In this vein, rectangular photographs gain more attention and are more convincing than other shapes, particularly irregular shapes. A single, dominant illustration will usually get more attention than multiple illustrations. However, a number of small illustrations scattered throughout the text can increase readership.

Now, pay attention to this: Many ads can depend on form rather than content because you really don't want them to say anything. Let's say you're having a dry spell at the shows and your latest group of puppies have not hit the ring yet. You want to advertise and keep your name in the limelight, but you have nothing to boast about. Now is the time to get clever and design an ad that holds the reader's attention but says nothing more specific than what great dogs you have.

Your goal in advertising is to get the readers to act as you want them to. You have to prove to them that you have a better whatsis than the other guy or that you can give them four for the price of three. Aim at their self interest. The more physical the better: "a chance to make money;" "show better taste;" "have better puppies;" "put up my dog and be secure you made the right decision." And you need to back it up with logic.

How can you get the proper reader reaction?

If you want to catch the attention of judges, you could cite all the outstanding judges who have put up your Special, thereby getting them to say to themselves: "If I do the same, I will be right in line with the big guys." This identification advertising can work well because it appeals to a group and it unifies people. Do it tastefully and in an understated manner. Don't try to hit judges over the head with hammers for they will resent your tactics and your effort will backfire.

Which medium should I use?

For breeding purposes, all-breed magazines and newspapers will probably not yield the serious breeder business you want. They might tend to reinforce the idea that your dog is successful and therefore has good conformation. But, they seldom produce stud services. Your breed magazine is the place to talk about you dog's outstanding pedigree and his descent from top-producing bloodlines.

Use your all-breed publication to emphasize your dog's winning ways and how popular he is in his breed. In the breed magazine, start by telling about the good bitches being bred to him, and as his pups hit the ground, talk about their winning ways, all the while pointing up your dog's latest show wins.

Surveys have shown that the best place for an ad, especially if it has a striking photo, is the upper right-hand side of a right-hand page when the magazine is fully opened. The dominance of the left hemisphere of the brain causes us to glance automatically at the right-hand side first.

If you are going for a full-page display, your best bet for greater attention is the right-hand page of the centerfold. You will find that some publications will charge more for this location. They, too, know this.

Let's face it. Most of us don't know the ins and outs of advertising. In fact, there is strong evidence from our reading of dog publications that many of us don't write very well. So, what makes you think you're going to be able to write and layout an ad that will SELL?

Being practical and, we hope, economical, it's best to get professional advice. Look in your local phone book or check with your newspapers and ask for someone with copywriting experience to look over your efforts. You want your ad to have punch.

You want words that describe. You want to make sure the reader realizes the benefits to them if they do what you ask of them.

Allow for ample "white space." Don't cram every photo you can into a restricted space and don't try to overwhelm with too many words. And, do not use regional expressions and expect a guy in Tucson to understand a New England colloquialism. And you Californians, cool it on the valley talk. Remember, it's best to say too little rather than too much. Following that advice has gotten a lot of presidents elected.

Most magazines will help you with layout. Sometimes, it's just best to give them your copy and photos and let them run with it, or at least until you know more.

When you plan your advertising and repeat it enough times to call attention to its contents, people should react. If you follow the guidelines enumerated above and develop a well-thought-through plan of attack and back it up with a sensible budget plan, it can make the difference between a successful career for your dog and your kennel and being an also-ran.

CHAPTER SUMMARY:

Advertising a non-product is a waste of money.

Promoting a dog's successful campaign could cost as much as handler's fees.

Most advertising fails.

Don't take an ad bigger than it need be.

Repetition of an ad increases recognition.

Plan your ad carefully to get the reaction you desire.

Place your ad in the most advantageous location in a publication.

The visuals of your ad are most important.

Money, Money, Where Does It All Go?

"is there a loss-leader
in the crowd?"

Few people entering the sport of showing and breeding purebred dogs have any idea what this hobby can cost per year. I know that collecting stamps and raising exotic fish can run into big dollars, but this hobby can be the runaway winner if you let it get out of control.

To the best of my knowledge, no one has published information on the cost of being involved in the dog show game. The major reason is that people get into the sport at different levels of commitment, and therefore spend widely differing amounts to satisfy their desire to compete.

In this chapter we'll give you some ballpark figures for varying size kennels and select levels of competition for you to chose so you can put together realistic budgets.

An important point to remember is that if you wish to become well known for your winning dogs, you cannot hide your light (and your dogs') under a rock, and that means spending money on advertising and promoting your good dogs. The magazine owners will come to love you.

If you reach the level where you're campaigning a top-winning dog on a regular basis, consider $25,000 a year to be about what it will cost you for that dog's campaign alone, and then add the costs for maintaining your ongoing show and breeding program. If you were involved with horses or racing power boats, it could cost you a great deal more. AG

Money bags

What are the major costs involved in showing dogs?

Your first major expenditure is the purchase of your basic stock. As was mentioned in an earlier chapter, it's best to start with a good male to gain experience. It's a lot easier convincing a top breeder to part with a good male than a quality bitch. Now, before we talk dollars you need to consider that first male as your experience dog.

This dog will be your entry to the shows and will open an avenue of continuing communication with the breeder. He will introduce you to all kinds of fascinating people who populate the dog show scene. He will give you joy, heartache, an opportunity to see the best in people, an opportunity to see the worst in people, and a chance to see parts of your state and country you might not normally see.

Fig. 8. Budget

LEVEL I		
3 dogs, 1 being shown, 2 at home		
	Year #1	Year #3	Year #5
---	---	---	---
Purchase stock: one show male, 2 good brood bitches	500	750	
Dog food (high quality)	330	350	375
Veterinary fees	350	600	565
AKC registration fees	48	6	6
Entry fees for 20 dog shows	300	300	300
Dog magazine, newspaper subscriptions	180	180	180
Travel to shows (25 days, transportation, meals, catalogs)	1,125	1,500	1,650
Overnight accommodations at shows (5 nights)	250	300	375
Win photographs (7)	186(10)	265(15)	398
Handler fees, 20 shows	1,300		
Ringside pickup			
No ringside, includes board		1,770	
Includes BB wins			2,130
Magazine, newspaper ads	200	650	1,050
Stud fees	–	150	250
Grooming, bathing equipment	150	50	–
Kennel facilities	350	2,500	200
RV purchase	–	–	–
Crates and tack boxes	550	75	–
Whelping pens	–	125	–
Purchase of additional stock (first good bitch)	–	1,200	–
Shipping bitches to be bred	–	250	350
Cost of raising a litter of 6 pups (excluding vet bills)	–	300	350
Costs of selling a litter (shots, advertising)	–	185	100
Purchase of breed books, other needed books	85	125	75
Membership fees in specialty all-breed clubs	25	75	85
Phone bills	360	530	750
Accountant fees	–	225	225
Taxes	–	–	–

LEVEL II
5 dogs, 2 campaigning, 3 at home
2 litters a year, extra to feed mothers and pups

	Year #1	Year #3	Year #5
Dog food (high quality)	625	650	675
Veterinary fees	625	750	750
AKC registration fees	92	12	12
Entry fees, 2 dogs, 15 shows each @$15	450	500	575
Dog magazine, newspaper subscriptions	180	180	180
Travel to shows (30 shows, transportation, meals, catalogs)	1,690	1,800	1,950
Overnight accommodations at shows (10 nights)	500	550	600
Win photographs (16)	425	425	425
Handler fees (2 BV wins)	2,150	2,300	2,500
Magazine, newspaper ads	650	1,000	1,250
Stud fees	300	375	500
Grooming, bathing equipment	150	100	–
Kennel facilities	2,500	150	50
RV purchase	–	–	–
Crates and tack boxes	550	50	–
Whelping pens	125	100	–
Purchase of additional stock (first good bitch)	1,200	–	–
Shipping bitches to be bred	250	175	225
Cost of raising 2 litters (excluding vet bills)	600	650	700
Costs of selling litters	370	185	150
Purchase of breed books, other needed books	85	50	50
Membership fees in specialty, all-breed clubs	75	75	75
Phone bills	450	450	450
Accountant fees	150	175	200
Taxes	–	–	–

LEVEL III
Campaign 1 Special & 2 Class dogs
7 dogs at home, 3 litters per year

	Year #1	Year #3	Year #5
Dog food (high quality)	1,095		
Veterinary fees	1,250		
AKC registration fees	160	18	18
Entry fees for dog shows (50 shows for Special, 15 each for Class dogs)	1,200	1,350	1,500
Dog magazine, newspaper subscriptions	180	180	180
Travel to 30 shows (transportation, meals, catalogs)	850	850	850
Overnight accommodations at shows	–	–	–
Win photographs (35 Special, 15 Class)	1,325	1,450	1,600
Handler fees (30 Class, 70 Special)	7,080	8,000	8,700
Magazine, newspaper ads	8,000	8,000	8,000
Stud fees	750	500	850
Grooming, bathing equipment	300	50	50
Kennel facilities	5,000	250	150
RV purchase ($36,000 cost, 10% interest)	4,500	4,500	4,500
Crates and tack boxes	800	50	50
Whelping pens	250	–	–
Shipping bitches to be bred	250	250	250
Cost of raising litters (excluding vet bills)	900	975	1,050
Costs of selling litters	525	300	200
Purchase of breed books, other needed books	85	50	50
Membership fees in specialty all-breed clubs	75	75	75
Phone bills	650	725	850
Accountant fees	250	300	350
Taxes	–	–	–

Back to costs! We will use a middle-sized breed, such as a Cocker Spaniel, as our model. A typical pet-quality Cocker should cost about $200 at eight weeks of age. Rarer breeds will cost more. Using this as a rule of thumb, expect to pay $500-$750 for a prospective show dog (male) at four months of age. If you're in the market for a Lakeland Terrier, for example, expect to pay somewhat more as this breed registers less than 1 percent of the Cocker's annual registration of 100,000 a year.

We've set up a list of things you need to consider when developing your budget. The matrix is based on Year 1, Year 3, and Year 5 using three levels of effort. Level One will be campaigning a single dog with two at the kennel. Level Two will be a modest effort typical of the average hobby breeder in which two dogs are campaigned during the year and five are at home and there is one litter a year. Level Three will be that of a fully committed breeder campaigning a top Specials, as well as showing two class dogs and having seven dogs at home with three litters a year.

Before you throw in the sponge, we'll tell you that the vast majority of breeder/exhibitors fall into the first two categories. We would guess this group's average yearly income to be 30-to-35-thousand dollars from their occupations or professions.

It's a fact of life that money can make a big difference in a dog's Specials campaign. A dog with money behind him will have the advantage that advertising and promotion can produce. We're not saying he wasn't a good dog to begin with – it's just that he will probably have an edge.

There are many people who love to be associated with the sport but don't want the work and planning it takes to have a top winner. Many of these people sponsor a dog. They assume partial ownership and pay the handling, advertising and transportation costs just so they can have their names listed as co-owners. It happens.

If you plan to get further involved with the sport, it would be wise to consult your accountant or tax attorney before filing your first tax returns and taking the dogs as a deduction. It depends upon whether you can prove it's not just a hobby before you are allowed to use it as an IRS deduction. Do this early, before you get yourself into trouble.

If you are going to set up your accounts as a business, don't forget to take depreciation on your equipment (check to see if you can take depreciation on your breeding stock).

Just to see you smile, We're going to list the ways you can offset some of the costs of your involvement in purebred dogs. First, the way most people recoup some of their investment is through sales of their litters. Just how much you can realize is a matter of breed, locale and value of the puppies. If they're the offspring of famous and successful stock, they should bring top dollar. If they are just good prospects, lower your sights, and if they turn out to be pet quality, remember, each sale helps.

Can I offset any of the costs?

No bitch should be bred more than once a year. This is your hobby not your livelihood. Do not become a puppy factory. For most of us, two litters a year is more than enough to care for and be sure they get into proper homes.

Another way of offsetting costs is to offer your dog at stud. Unless your dog turns out to be a top winner and a prolific sire, the amount of money you will see as income is small. Be selective, breed him to good bitches and keep him in good shape. Then take the money.

CHAPTER SUMMARY:

The sport of showing and breeding purebred bogs can be expensive.

Your first major expenditure is the purchase of your stock.

It's wise to prepare a realistic budget.

The average yearly income of breeders/exhibitors is $30-35 thousand.

You can help offset your costs through stud fees and the sale of puppies.

11

The Arbiters

"insights and hindsights"

If you are going to be a winner, you need to understand how a judge does his job and where he's coming from. Judges are human, believe it or not, and they have their likes and dislikes just like you and me. They also come from different backgrounds: Many are former handlers who were quite successful in their chosen occupations; many are doctors, lawyers, vets, businessmen or other professions. They mostly have one thing in common – success in their fields.

Maybe this is true because they are used to making critical decisions. So, by and large, the fact that they can make critical decisions and are successful because they most often make the right ones, their feelings of competence are reinforced.

If you understand this, you can make it work for you. Judges are successful people and they recognize and appreciate other competent and successful people. Act the part. Walk into the ring as if your dog is the "livin' end." He should be trained, as suggested earlier, and radiate confidence. Carry yourself as if you were proud of what you are doing and most important, dress the part.

Pay close attention to the judge's ring directions and carry them out correctly and with alacrity. If you understand this and the insights into judges' psyches that follow, you should do very well in the show ring. I've written this chapter to help you understand judges and judging. AG

Judge Derek Rayne pointing

As you have probably noticed, dog show exhibitors are very competitive and many are quite emotional. Frankly, it takes a very strong, objective personality to stand in the ring and judge dogs, and then, having done so, turn a deaf ear to the sore losers and would-be slanderers.

Fortunately, for the exhibitors, this kind of judge is in the majority and will continue to receive assignments and draw large entries, thereby getting the opportunity to become even more proficient and knowledgeable. On the other hand, the judge who is intimidated by big-name handlers and exhibitors can become indecisive and in a whole peck of trouble. If this type of judge does not overcome his problems and learn to judge dogs, he will either become a drop-out or will receive fewer and fewer assignments.

Many of the top show dogs are highly publicized in print, and because judges receive these magazines and newspapers free they are quite aware of who's who. Spectators and competitors gather at ringside to see these dogs do battle. The stresses of competition at ringside and in the ring are frequently strained to the breaking point as tensions mount and emotions erupt. It is imperative that with all of this going on, the judge remain removed from this extraneous pressure and judge the dogs according to the standards.

Unfortunately, it is when a judge does not use good judgment that things begin to deteriorate and the prevailing stresses encircle the show ring and intrude at center stage. It is at this point that a number of things can happen:

1. The wrong end of the lead becomes important;
2. A dog's record, if known, overcomes a judge's judging ability;
3. A particular exhibitor known to the judge makes his presence felt;
4. An impression is created that the dog needs only these points to finish, whether he does or not (this is one of the oldest gimmicks of them all).

In point of fact, there are many ways an inept judge can be manipulated. But, this does not necessarily make him dishonest; no, it is more likely at this point that he is intimidated.

From talking to many of my fellow judges, I know that feelings are hurt when their decisions are criticized. No one, exhibitor or judge, likes to be put down. In my judgment, the major consolation of any good judge is the long-term record. It is best to evaluate how well the dogs he has placed have done under other reputable judges. How consistent have they been?

An extremely important point, often forgotten, is that competent judges can teach exhibitors the direction in which to go with their breeding programs, and it is for exhibitors to study their dogs' placements for guidance. Whether you win or lose, please try to take the judge's decisions in a constructive light and try to learn from each one.

I remember very well how in my early dog show days I would become especially "ticked" with a judge when my pride and joy wasn't put up. I vowed never to show under that crooked judge again. However, as time passed, I began to recognize that many of the dogs these judges put up were equally recognized by judges I respected. Once I was able to swallow my anger and pride, I began to withhold judgment on a single assignment of a given judge and look at his performance over a period of time.

We have learned that a good class dog will win three out of five shows or 60 percent of the time. If you check the show placements in the AKC Gazette, you will find these dogs "in the ribbons" even when they don't win.

Winning is an exhilarating experience – losing ain't! But there are times when getting the right colored ribbons isn't everything. Winners and losers are determined by one person's comparisons and interpretations of a written standard. Watching a competent judge at work can be a rewarding experience. Watch the hands come back to areas of weakness and strength, observe the sorting out of like specimens and the rechecking of comparable features of the group. Watch, watch, watch – it can be like a verbal critique.

For further insights into judges and judging, let's follow a typical judge through a part of his assignment:

"OK, here comes another class of Golden Retrievers. So far, the Puppy and Bred by Exhibitor classes haven't shown me anything really great. Let's hope the Open class has some quality. First, check off the arm bands – one absent out of 11. Now, let's have a look. Hmm, that third dog, the dark red one doesn't look too bad, however, that dark color isn't favored. The next-to-last dog looks pretty good overall; let's see if he hangs together when he moves. Nothing much else at first look. Let's send them around the ring and look at toplines, reach and drive. Whoa, that number 5 dog just came alive. He didn't look like much stacked, but look at that baby move out. He is possibly going to be the one to beat.

"Now, let's go over them individually. The first two don't differ from my first impression, nothing here. The dark one is nicely balanced, an 11/12 height-length ratio. Looks about the right weight, too. Moves out all right. Slightly close in the rear and just begins to single track coming back. The chest is a bit wide, maybe a 7 on a scale of 10, but not bad.

'The number 4 dog shouldn't be here. No class, no style. Bones put together correctly, but the dog is just lacking overall.

"Now, for the number 5 dog. Head OK, eyes a bit light, ears set properly, good skull and expression. Shoulders are a bit steep. I would like a little more width in front but the chest is down to the elbows and the elbows themselves are placed correctly. No evidence of barbering. You know, I sort of prefer the whiskers trimmed...oh well, the standard says either way. Neck blends a bit roughly into the shoulders, those darn shoulders! Good spring of ribs, I would say the body is a bit long – say 11/13. Good coat texture, tail set on all right, the angle at croup OK. Let's step back a bit from this guy and have another look. What is it about him that bothers me? I saw him move and he was a world beater. Standing here, he looks just better than average. Why can he move like that? Let's see, rear angulation is a bit more than in front. Hmm, I'll come back to him again. Let's say for now a 7 or an 8 – a contender here.

"Dogs 6 through 8, not much to commend them. Not bad dogs, just not good enough. Now, for that next-to-last dog. Overall, he looks in balance, nothing exceptional, nothing bad. Best thing about him is that all parts fit together. He moves OK, too. No fireball, but no slouch either. Got a good handler on him – Hey! come on, let's not think like that. Well, why not? The guy knows how to put down a dog right. Forget it! Judge the dog.

"Finally, the last dog in the class. A fair one, probably in the ribbons in this competition, but not my winner. I like him and should give him a piece of the pie. However, today, and in this competition, he ain't going to make it.

"There they are. Just waiting for me to send a signal. Let's see, the dark-colored one, while not favored, is not a disqualification either. However, the Golden video program didn't tout this color. Still, he is quite a dog overall. My number 5 showman is undoubtedly the best mover in this class and would make a deserving winner. My next-to-last dog could make it too. OK, OK, let's get on the stick. Time to make a decision – move them around the ring. For better or for worse, I'll take the dark-colored one. It will benefit the breed in the long run. Number two to my showing bomb, number three to my next-to-last, and number four to the last one in the class. Any second thoughts – nope, that's it. I can live with it.

"Where did that wind come from? Wouldn't you know, I left my sweater in my bag and it's in the trunk of the show chairman's car and she is nowhere to be seen. Boy! I hope the club treasurer is around when I need him.

"Here comes the Open bitch class in Gordons. Six of them. No puppies or other classes. Oh boy, I'm going to have my work cut out for me here. They all look different. How can I be consistent in what I put up when there is no consistency in what is presented. I need to remind myself to talk to the AKC rep about the wording in the Judges Handbook – consistency, indeed.

"That first bitch looks nice and I guess structurally she is acceptable. However, if you dyed her a dark red, she could pass as an acceptable Irish. According to my book, this class is for Gordons only. So? So, she ain't correct breed type, that's what. You don't place her if you have others to use. Yeah, but she looks sound. Look dummy, breed type is important, remember? OK, OK, let's get on with it.

"Number 2 looks fair to middling. She sure feels hard. Moves well, too. Sometimes those tan markings sure can make it look like they are crossing over in front when they are really single tracking. Little too much droop in the croup.

"Number 3 is a point maker. Another one that fades from memory. Nothing really bad, but shows no spark, no animation and she has no outstanding characteristics. Can't say she is balanced, but neither is she, what word am I searching for? Oh well, unbalanced. Who knows, I just know that this one ain't it.

"Now, Number 4 is a nice one. Moves like she's enjoying it. She has that sparkle. Like it all lights up and looks good. I guess I could nitpick...in fact, I see some minor problems, but I like her overall. She has her act together. This gal's got it unless I find a better one.

"Number 5 is going to be in there. Color is a bit light. Good head, very good head. I like her blend of neck and shoulders. Look at her move out – straight and true. Well, maybe number 4 hasn't got a lock on this one yet. Good bitch, she is going to give me complications.

"The handler on number 6, old Jocko Carnes, is having a tough time with his bitch. Now, Jocko and I go back a long way together. He 'specialed' my famous B/T, and we had some great times together. Old Jocko hasn't been doing too well lately. He sure could use some winners. Now he's got her steady. OK, let's have a look. Not bad at all, I like her, too. Just a shade long and her hip bones are quite pronounced. Let's see her move. Well, Jocko, you have a pretty fair one there. All right, leads on. Let's see them go around. This is a tough one. I like Jocko's bitch, but numbers 5 and 4 – oh, come on, number 4 you've got it, Jocko's bitch is second, and number 5 is third. That's the way it goes. You know, I'm getting hungrier by the minute.

"A quick sip of coffee (cold by now) and in comes black Cocker Spaniels. I love them, but all that coat! I feel like a voice from the wilderness when I tell them I am penalizing their dog for excessive or wrong-textured coats. That's the only kind of coat most of the exhibitors have ever seen.

"This looks like a promising 6-9 class. Five entries in all. And all, from this perspective, look like they could win it. Let's take a look at their heads, hmmm, I'd like a little more foreface on all of them. Nice earsets, good toplines stacked – in fact, too good. Let me correct this one. She has him stretched so far that his back looks like the angle on a ski jump. There, he looks like a dog again. Nice coats, decent bone and substance. Let's move them. Oh, Oh, there goes the topline on numbers 1 and 3. Number 2 has his rump higher than his withers. The other two look all right. Of course, if they didn't jump up and down like the puppies they are it would be a lot easier to see them better.

"OK, first one up on the table. Oops, a mouth only a mother could love. Nice bone and substance. Moves with a terrier tail, means the croup angle is probably wrong. The second little one is cute. He is a bit small for me but he may be at the young end of the class range. Moves all right. Looks like he would rather roll over and play. Perhaps if the handler didn't use the squeaky toy so much he might settle down more.

"Number 3, forget it. This little fellow has big troubles. His stifles feel like jelly and he wobbles as he moves away from me. Poor little guy.

"Number 4 is all leg and little body development. Boy, how puppies differ in their development. So, what do you want from a six-month-old baby? He is serious about the showing bit though. Look at him stack on the table. Doesn't move too badly either. Bone structure is right except for a steeper shoulder than I would like to see.

"Now, on to number 5. This kid is an eater. I bet he beat his littermates to the chow bowl every night. Nice little puppy, though. Has all the right things – they just roll and shake. This little fellow has this class hands down. He means business and he moves straight and true. Let's give him the blue with number 2 second.

"As I look at my watch, I see that it's 2:39 and they are calling the first group. Boy, my back is hurting and I didn't sleep too good last night. On top of that, the service at the motel restaurant wasn't exactly speedy this morning, so I just had time to wolf down some cold cereal before we had to leave for the fairgrounds. Lunch? Well, let's think about other things. Maybe I can grab a sandwich at the airport before my red-eye flight home.

Let's see, what else's left to judge. Irish Water Spaniels and Irish Setters. Good thing the entries are small. It looks like I'm on time, averaging about 24 dogs an hour. I still can't fathom why it's so all-fired important to judge at this pace. I wish I had more time to give some of the tougher classes...well, no AKC rep in sight, so I must be on schedule.

"There's Mary at ringside. I wonder if she has an entry in the Irishs coming up. No matter...just wondering. My, how my mind can wander at times. I wonder if other judges have the same problem?"

There are many, many reasons why people apply for judges' licenses, not the least of which is ego enhancement. And there's nothing wrong with that. All of us like to feel important. It's a great feeling to walk into the ring and know that all eyes are on you and that you have important and serious work to do. How we react to the challenge is the crux of this section.

Why do people become judges?

I'm going to presuppose that judges have spent many years as breeders preparing themselves for this responsibility and have studied the breeds for which they are licensed. Given these conditions, let's walk into the ring with three mythical judges.

Judge #1: Mrs. Hortense Affremo has had a noted career in her own breed. She and her husband have bred more than 30 champions and campaigned the best ones extensively with a good handler. The Affremos live quite comfortably in the suburbs enjoying an excellent living.

Hortense was raised in a big city by middle-class parents. She managed to attend a good college nearby where she met Bud Affremo, also a struggling student. Together they planned how they would tackle the world and conquer it.

About five years into their marriage, Hortense and Bud decided to start a family. Hortense settled down to the life of a suburban housewife and mother. However, something was missing. She needed an identity of her own.

You guessed it. A friend down the street raised Cairn Terriers. After some coffee klatches, at which showing dogs was the main topic of conversation, Hortense became smitten by the idea of showing her own dogs. This was a chance to find her place in the sun. She would prove herself to everyone; she would become the great breeder, and everyone would have to acknowledge that she radiated a light of her own. And you know what? She did it. She showed everyone, including her too-busy husband.

Judge #2. Alfred P. Bighouse grew up during the Great Depression. He had only few toys but realized that money was needed for food, rent, clothing and other essentials.

He did feel frustrated and deprived, however. His bicycle, when he had one, was always a used one that could be purchased for a couple of bucks. His fielder's mitt was always some other kid's throwaway. He saved forever to buy ice skates. When he got them, he was never completely satisfied because they weren't really what he wanted, just what he could afford.

Alfred grew into a man and forgot all those childish things – or thought he did. Except that when he was making a fairly good living, he spent his money on unusual things, such as fancy cars and expensive toys for adults. Everybody he knew chuckled about it.

When he became enthralled with the dog show craze, he bought and campaigned top-winning show dogs. He joined dog clubs. He really didn't enjoy this much, but it was important to him to do it. He applied for a judge's license because it implied status.

Judge #3. Byron G. Maxwether was a quiet child who loved to read. His parents were well off and he was raised in a comfortable home. Byron had no close childhood friends. He was studious and excelled in debate in high school and college. He didn't date much and was uncomfortable with girls his own age.

After establishing himself as a patent attorney, he met and married Maxine, a widow five years older with three small children.

Byron and Maxine became interested in dogs after being encouraged to show their purebred boxer at a local match. When he placed fourth in a class of four, the Maxwethers wanted to know why. After talking to breeders and attending local shows, they gradually came to appreciate the finer points of the breed.

They developed a 10-year plan for success. By the end of this period, they had bred seven champions and had a good reputation for sound stock. They were hooked.

Three years later, Byron began to judge at matches and sweepstakes and found that he enjoyed it. He was approved to judge in due course and has had five assignments to date.

Here we have three licensed judges ready to step

into the ring at the Queen of Sheba Kennel Club. As you have seen, they come from very diverse backgrounds. Although they have been evaluated and granted licenses by AKC, they may, because of their backgrounds, perform quite differently under similar circumstances. Let's see if we can determine why.

Rather than try to use "pop" psychology to explain the actions of our judges, I am going to draw upon the work of one of our nation's top think tanks – SRI International of Menlo Park, California.

SRI developed a "Values and Lifestyles" or VALS theory to classify types of American adults into nine distinct patterns. Originally developed to assist firms in marketing, this theory has been found to be useful for a variety of other purposes.

At the bottom of the VALS typology is the Need-Driven group consisting of two sets of money-restricted consumers, Survivors and Sustainers.

Survivors tend to be old, poor and depressed, those who are far removed from the cultural mainstream. Very few judges come from this group.

Sustainers are relatively young and struggle at the edge of poverty. Many are female heads of households. Sustainers are willing to do anything to get ahead. Again, few judges come from this category.

By far the most Americans belong to the Outer-Directed grouping, which includes the Belongers, Emulators and Achievers. They conduct their lives in accordance with what they think other people will think of them.

Belongers are traditional, conservative, puritanical and unexperimental people who would rather blend into a crowd than stand out. Their homes are their castles, and their ideas are the ideas of those around them. This is a predominantly white, middle-class, middle-aged grouping. Belongers comprise the mass market you hear so much about.

Emulators are ambitious, upwardly mobile, status-conscious, competitive people who are trying to break into the system. They are forever trying to keep up with the Joneses. They tend to be distrustful and angry, with little faith they will get a fair shake from the establishment.

Achievers are those who have made it, the leaders in business, the professions and government. They have fame, status and comfort.

The VALS research indicates that the one group of Americans expected to grow is the Inner-Directed category, including the I-Am-MEs, Experimental and Societally Conscious.

The I-Am-MEs, many of whom are children of Achievers, are exhibitionist, narcissistic, impulsive, fiercely individualistic and profoundly inventive. As the I-Am-MEs mature, many become Experimental, displaying a bent for direct experience and vigorous involvement in the world around them. These folks are artistic, experimental and highly participative. They are willing to do almost anything once.

Next come the Societally Conscious, who are attracted to simple living and smallness of scale. They tend to support such causes as conservation, environmentalism and consumerism. They tend to have slightly more money than the Experimentals, which they spend on favorite causes and solar heating.

The last group into which American adults fall is the Integrateds. This rare breed combines the power of outer-directedness with the sensitivity of inner-directedness. The SRI research indicates that only about 2 percent of the population falls into this category, which makes the group of little statistical importance and one not analyzed in detail by SRI.

Okay, now back to the judges.

Mrs. Affremo, as you may have surmised, is a Belonger, the group known as the huge stabilizing force in our country. They are by nature conservative, conventional and unexperimental. She does not perceive herself in this manner, however. She fully believes she can walk into the ring and make solid objective judgments.

Mr. Bighouse, as an Emulator, lives in a wholly different world from the other two judges. He is quite status conscious, macho and competitive and tends to be leery of getting a fair shake from the powers that be. He is not aware of this. Mr. Bighouse truly believes he cannot be swayed except by the facts.

Mr. Maxwether is a far different cookie from

either of his fellow judges. His group, the Achievers, are leaders in business, the professions and government. Achievers are able and affable people who created the system in response to the American Dream. Mr. Maxwether has no doubt whatever that he can make efficient and correct decisions based on the merits of the dogs he judges.

There are two highly advertised and promoted champions in the Specials class. What's going on in the judges' minds?

For Mrs. Affemo, selecting one of them is only natural. They are obviously good, everyone has put them up, and it's a safe decision.

Mr. Bighouse is gazing at that flashy puppy he put winners dog. This dog could go on to be one of the great winners of the breed and he discovered him and gave him his first big sendoff.

Mr. Maxwether isn't sure in his own mind. Those two Specials look really good, but the puppy has strong points too. Let's take them around again and let the winner pick himself.

Three judges, three honest persons, three points of view! No, judging isn't crooked. Yes, there are differences between judges. But as you have seen, there are differences between people who are not dog show judges. These diverse backgrounds help the sport. They help provide for differences in type. Good dogs, regardless of type, win under most judges. Now, if we could only pre-identify what group a judge belongs to we might be able to post a higher percentage of wins. "Where did you say you put that old psychology book?"

CHAPTER SUMMARY:

Judges come from varied backgrounds, although nearly all of them have been breeders/exhibitors.

To be successful in the dog show game, exhibitors need to understand the psychology of judges.

Competent judges can teach exhibitors which directions to take in their breeding programs.

PART III
BREEDING

12 How to Breed Winning and Producing Dogs

"this is where
you want to be"

In this chapter we will acquaint you with the basics of heredity and the science of genetics. For more in-depth coverage of the subject, you should read *The Standard Book of Dog Breeding: A New Look* (Dr. Alvin Grossman, Doral Publishing, 1991) and *Genetics for Dog Breeders* (Frederick B. Hutt, W.H. Freeman & Co., 1979).

It's important to realize that you won't go far as a breeder if you don't understand the basic facts about genetics. You may, as some have before you, get lucky and produce very good dogs for awhile. However, not understanding how you did it will prevent you from sustaining "your line" for any period of time. Behind any great line of dogs are great bitches. They are worth their weight in gold.

To some breeders, having an eye for a dog is second nature. Breeders lacking this natural talent can become self-taught provided they have the intelligence and motivation to discern between the good and poor examples set before them.

Consistent breeding of top, show dogs depends upon other important factors besides the natural or acquired talents of the breeder. Unfortunately, many breeders still operate under the illusion that second best will produce as well as the choice specimen – pedigrees being equal. Yeah! Maybe lady luck will come through every once in awhile, but choosing second best leads to nothing but heartbreak. Don't try it. Please.

Now, for those of you who believe in the "crapshoot" theory of the universe, I do have some reassuring words. A most important element contributing to the success or failure of any breeding program is that of chance or luck. Everything else being equal, sex distribution, puppy mortality, timing, the transmission of the best, or poorest, genes depend heavily on lady luck. However, there is a definite pattern to inherited traits and established ratios you can count on. More about this later.

The first step in any animal-breeding program is to decide what is ideal in your breed. You have to read and understand your breed standard, observe as many different dogs in the ring as you can and "yak" away at as many breeders as you can, describing what you have seen and what you like. Get their feedback.

Until you know what your ideal "boomer hound" looks like in your mind's eye, you are stopped cold and can neither select the best nor discard the worst. This is where the breeder's capabilities and talents come into play. This is the basis of selective breeding, which is the backbone of any successful breeding program. AG

What is "genetics?"

The science of genetics studies the process of heredity: how reproduction determines the characteristics of offspring; how those characteristics are distributed among offspring; and, how environment contributes to the shaping of hereditary characteristics. Gregor Mendel, a 19th Century monk, is considered to be the founder of genetics. He proved that traits are passed – with mathematical precision – from one generation to the next.

Mendel postulated certain mathematical ratios by which factors were inherited. For a simple, single characteristic like coat, the formula was 3:1. Three dominant colors to one recessive when the recessive color was present in both of the original pair. If the mated pair has one dominant color and one recessive color, then the resulting offspring are all of the dominant color.

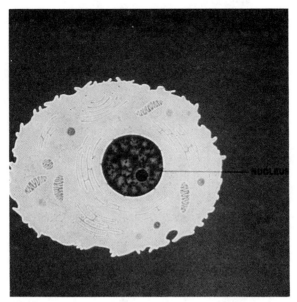

Nucleus

A gene is the smallest unit of hereditary information; a given gene might help determine skin color, height, or intelligence. People – and dogs, as well – have thousands and thousands of genes.

How are traits passed from parent to offspring?

Genes are part of a chromosome, a long strand of matter contained in each cell nucleus. A dog's cells contain 39 pairs of chromosomes, or a total of 78. Chromosomes are made up of strands of protein and a substance known as DNA. Sections of DNA strands are called genes.

The center of a cell is called a nucleus. The instructions for most cells' activities come from small structures in the nucleus, the chromosomes. When a cell reaches a certain size, it may divide into two cells. Before this happens, each chromosome makes a perfect copy of itself. As the cell divides, one chromosome moves to one side of the cell, while its duplicate moves to the other side. The two new cells then have exactly the same kind and number of chromosomes as the original cell.

We have learned that each specimen contains a pair of genes for each trait it inherits, in each of its

Fig. 9. The 3:1 Ratio

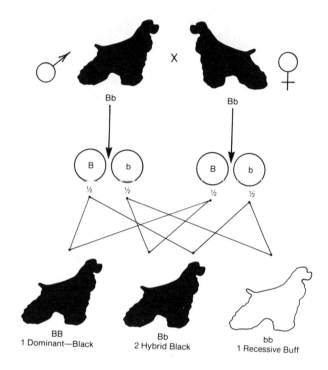

cells, one contributed by the sire and one by the dam. Using a dominant black and a buff Cocker Spaniel as our example, all the first generation will be the dominant color. But, many of them are not really dominant blacks, but hybrids, which means having the ability to produce the buff color when mated to another hybrid. OK, so let's take two black hybrids, .mate them and see what we get. Every hybrid can pass on to each of its offspring either the black or the buff characteristics.

Therefore, the transmission of one or the other has a 50/50 chance. It's possible to predict not only the possible combination of factors, but also the probability for each of the combinations. Here we get one dominant black, two hybrid black and one buff – three black and one buff, or Mendel's 3:1 ratio.

Let's move from the inheritance of a single trait to the inheritance of two traits simultaneously.

By breeding a homozygous (pure) black dog that is tall (also homozygous) to a short buff specimen that is also pure for its traits, we will get tall, black offspring, since the traits are dominant. They are exactly like the black parent, black and tall.

Now, when you take these hybrid offspring, which are hybrid tall and hybrid black, and mate them with other like specimens, the resultant types are quite interesting. There will be four different types produced:. a small, black type and a tall, buff one. These types are new combinations of the two traits.

Continuing in this vein, and for all other traits as well, the distribution ratio turns out to be 9:3:3:1.

Fig. 10. The 9:3:1 Ratio

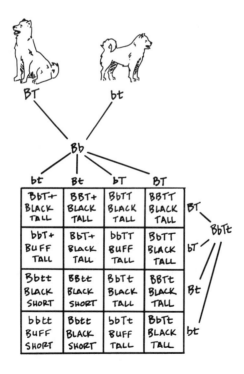

This means for every nine tall, black dogs in a hybrid X hybrid mating, there will be three tall dogs with buff coats, three small dogs with black coats and one, short buff specimen.

A quick glance will show 12 tall dogs to four short ones and 12 blacks to four buffs. Both demonstrate the 3:1 ratio already established for the inheritance of a single trait.

Hereditary characteristics are determined at conception. When offspring are conceived, a random selection of half of the father's genes combine with half of the mother's genes to comprise the offspring's genes. Thus, the number of possible combinations of genes is virtually limitless.

Only a few aspects of inheritance are controlled by a single pair of genes, and only a few more are controlled by two pairs. Most traits are determined by many genes. The cumulative effect of all these genes working together is a bewildering maze; only a few learned scientists can even begin to comprehend the genetic code, so don't sweat it.

How does genetics apply to dog breeding?

For the purposes of dog breeding, it is sufficient to understand the following statements:

1. Some traits are dominant, others are recessive. For example, in some breeds a black coat is dominant over a buff coat.

2. It is impossible to tell what traits are dominant by looking at the dog. For example, "tallness" is dominant over "shortness," but it is impossible to tell if a tall dog is homozygous or heterozygous (non-pure) for this trait.

3. The only proof of a dog's genetic makeup is in its offspring. For example, if a tall dog always produces tall offspring, you can be sure that it is homozygous for "tallness." If, however, some of its offspring are short, it is undoubtedly heterozygous for "tallness."

4. Another way of deducing a dog's genetic makeup is by studying its ancestors. For example, if a dog has a beautiful head, and if all of his male ancestors also had beautiful heads, then the dog's male offspring are also likely to display this trait.

5. Genetic factors set the dog's potential, but

Good head

environmental factors determine if a dog reaches that potential. For example, a dog may be genetically predisposed to "tallness." However, if the dog receives inadequate nutrition, he will never achieve his potential maximum height.

Inbreeding refers to the mating of two, closely related individuals. In the breeding of domestic animals, such as cattle and chickens, inbreeding is regarded as a valuable tool to fix (make dominant) a desired type and to purify a strain. By combining inbreeding with the selection of those individuals most nearly ideal in appearance and temperament, the desired stability of stock is quickly obtained.

Most dog breeders practice inbreeding to a limited

What is inbreeding?

extent, even though they may call it "close line-breeding." Actually, the breeding of half-brother to half-sister, as well as niece to uncle, or nephew to aunt, are limited forms of inbreeding. For purposes of this discussion, however, inbreeding will refer to the mating of full-brother to full-sister, father to daughter, and son to mother. Most breeders probably consider these three situations as representative of true inbreeding.

Does inbreeding cause degeneration of stock?

Most of the studies of inbreeding show that the decline in vigor, including the extinction of certain lines, follows the fixing of recessive genes that are injurious to the breed. However, along with the fixing of such recessives, there is also a fixing of traits that are beneficial and desirable. It is mostly a matter of chance as to what combination of genes a family finally comes to possess. The process of natural selection is always at work weeding out combinations that are not well adapted to the conditions of life.

There is a common belief that inbreeding causes monstrosities and defects, but evidence indicates that inbreeding itself has no specific connection with the occurrence of abnormalities. Rather, inbreeding seems merely to surface the genetic traits inherent in the original stock. Inbreeding does not create problems or virtues, it merely uncovers them.

Sometimes, abnormal or stillborn animals are produced if undesirable genes are carried in the stock. If an undesirable trait does show up in a litter, the breeder should know that it was already present in the hereditary make-up of the stock.

On the positive side, inbreeding degeneration is of such a peculiar nature that it may be totally abolished by a single breeding with unrelated or distantly related animals. This type of breeding is called "outcrossing." When an inbred dog is outcrossed, many of its undesirable, recessive traits will be negated by dominant genes from the other dog; the offspring should be vigorous and healthy. (For an illustration of the benefits of outcrossing, please read the introduction to Chapter 17, in which I describe my experience with slowly degenerating stock and the positive effect of a single outcrossing upon my dogs' bloodline.)

Fig. 11. Backcrossing

Pioneer   Mildred

Beatrix   Lovely

Pioneer   Lovely

Breeding the offspring of the father-to-daughter-mating or the son-to-mother-mating back to a parent is called "backcrossing." To illustrate this, suppose an outstanding male specimen is produced and the

Are some types of inbreeding more beneficial than others?

Fig. 12. Inbreeding

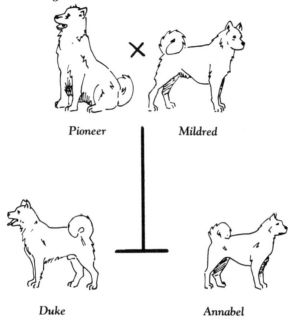

Pioneer ✕ Mildred

Duke   Annabel

Duke   Annabel

Pioneer Recreated

Fig. 13. Close Linebreeding

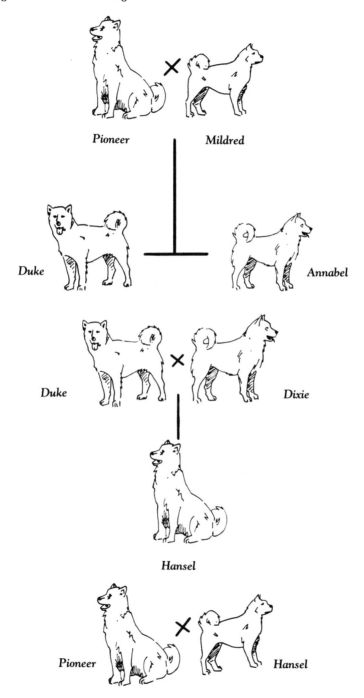

Pioneer   Mildred

Duke   Annabel

Duke   Dixie

Hansel

Pioneer   Hansel

breeder wishes to obtain more of the same type: The excellent male is bred back to his mother, and the breeder retains the best bitch puppies in the resulting litter.

By breeding these bitches back to their father, the excellent male, there is a good chance that some of the puppies produced will greatly resemble the outstanding sire. In backcrossing to a superior dog, it is improbable that there will be degeneration in the offspring.

Producing this superior inbred dog has many advantages to a breeder. It means that this specimen has a greater chance of passing on his visible traits rather than possible hidden traits. In the parlance of computer desktop publishing, this is called WYSIWYG – what you see is what you get. Prepotent dogs and bitches are usually those that are pure for many of their characteristics.

Since such a limited amount of line-breeding has been carried on in most breeds, prepotent specimens have become pure for certain traits more or less by chance, for they have appeared in all breeds as products of outcrossing, as well as line-breeding.

Because line-breeding, and especially close line-breeding, is a limited form of inbreeding, the same good and bad points apply to line-breeding, but in a much more modified degree. The practice of inbreeding appears to be extremely limited in dogs so one must assume that breeders are willing to trade slower progress for a lower element of risk with respect to degeneration.

The mating of full-brother to full-sister is the most intense form of inbreeding. This match is far more likely than backcrossing to produce inbreeding degeneration. Studies show that those breeders who have attempted this type of cross, for the purpose of fixing good characteristics in their stock, obtain inconsistent results. The resulting offspring typically display decreased vitality and robustness.

CHAPTER SUMMARY:

The science of genetics is the study of heredity, which is the distribution of characteristics among offspring.

Characteristics in offspring are determined by pairs of genes, with each parent providing one gene in each pair.

Some characteristics are dominant, or homozygous, while others are recessive, or heterozygous. Dominant characteristics always dominate over recessive characteristics.

Only a few characteristics are controlled by a single pair of genes; most are controlled by multiple pairs of genes.

Inbreeding is the breeding of closely related relatives, such as full-sister to full-brother, father to daughter, or mother to son. The breeding of niece to uncle, nephew to aunt, or half-brother to half-sister is a limited form of inbreeding, sometimes called line-breeding.

Inbreeding does not cause problems or produce virtues, rather it merely uncovers them and makes them a fixed trait.

"Backcrossing" occurs when a dog is bred back to its parent. Backcrossing generally yields positive results.

"Outcrossing" occurs when a dog is bred to an unrelated or distantly related dog. Outcrossing can abolish undesirable traits which have become fixed in a bloodline.

The Ultimate Test of the Breeders Art

"making the right breeding"

An *eye for a dog* is probably the most important thing a breeder needs. Without it, there is a lot of hard work ahead.

What do I mean by an eye for a dog? Let me draw an analysis for you. When my wife goes shopping she flips through acres of dresses on racks. To me, they look like floppy things on hangers. To her, knowing her measurements and what color and style flatter her build, it's easy for her to visualize the necessary accessories to finish the outfit. You, as a breeder, need to know the same sort of things: What kind of build you want your puppies to have; what should their color be; what accessories, texture and length of coat, ear set, etc., do you want.

You have to be able to visualize the sire and dam and their parents and grandparents. Then you can create by breeding one almost like the ones you have visualized, or capitalize on key features a grandparent had, and you want and see in your bitch. It's up to you to shape the next generation of winners and at the same time put your individual stamp on the breed.

Being artistic helps – not that you have to be able to paint a masterpiece on canvas, but you should be able to visualize and verbalize your ideal dog.

A truly meaningful pedigree is also a great asset in creating your ideal dog. A meaningful pedigree contains pictures and accurate information about each ancestor in at least the first three generations. All and any information should be included that gives you a better picture of your dog's ancestors. AG

How can a
pedigree help me
select a sire and
dam?

The pedigree of a purebred dog is a document that lists the dog's parents, grandparents, and so forth, usually going back five generations. In addition, most pedigrees list the dog's date of birth, the American Kennel Club registration number, and the breeder's name.

A pedigree, if interpreted correctly, can aid the skillful breeder in producing better specimens. The list of the dog's ancestors can be used, to a limited degree, as an indicator of what kind of offspring the dog will produce: offspring of two high-quality, top-producing parents are likely to be high-quality and top-producing. However, the only tangible proof of a dog's ability to produce quality will be seen in the puppies.

In interpreting a pedigree that contains only names, experienced breeders have an advantage over novices, for they have undoubtedly seen many of the specimens listed. To the novice breeder, pedigrees can be a confusing genealogical puzzle; but, experienced breeders can fill in, from firsthand knowledge, information about each dog's physical "type," personality, and producing power. The ability to understand a dog's pedigree comes after many years of observing a given breed.

Don't despair, it's not as hopeless as it may seem, however. With the assistance of a more experienced breeder, or through research, you can learn to decipher the relevant genetic information in a pedigree.

What is the
most important
characteristic to
look for in a
pedigree?

When selecting a mate for your dog, the most important aspect of the pedigree is the producing power (the ability to pass on superior traits) of each of the dog's ancestors. The offspring of superior parents are more likely to be top-quality producers than are excellent, individual dogs that lack a superior genetic background. Therefore, when analyzing a pedigree, keep in mind that it is not enough to have famous sires and dams as ancestors. It is also necessary that the ancestor's offspring were top producers, so that the qualities of those famous dogs can be passed to succeeding generations.

For example, suppose you are trying to choose

between two studs for your bitch. The first, Ziggy, comes from an excellent background. Most of his ancestors were top-quality dogs and have proven their ability to reproduce their good traits. Ziggy displays the characteristics that are dominant in his family. The second dog, Champion Patooty, is the top-winning dog of the day. He is an excellent individual physical specimen, but he lacks a solid genetic family background. Neither his sire nor his dam comes from a line of top-producing dogs. He is, against all odds, a genetic fluke. Which should you breed to your bitch? Even though Champion Patooty demands a higher stud fee, and even though you could boast about him at the next dog club meeting, the better choice is Ziggy. Ziggy is much more likely to contribute higher quality genes to your intended litter.

Unfortunately, most situations are not as clearly defined as this example. In addition to the separate genetic background of each parent, you must also consider how these backgrounds will combine. For example, mating a "bear-type" male Golden Retriever to a "sporting-type" female could yield undesirable results, even if both parents have excellent genetic backgrounds.

The great majority of dogs and bitches are probably dominant for some of their traits and not especially dominant for others. It is up to the breeder to match the proper combination of dominant traits, to make certain that the parents complement each other.

What combination of genetic makeup should I look for when choosing a sire and a dam?

There are some dogs and bitches that are completely non-dominant when bred to a dominant partner. In these matches, a number of dogs and bitches in a breed have produced top-quality offspring when they themselves were of lesser quality.

When a non-dominant bitch is bred to a non-dominant stud, the resulting litter is almost always a disappointment. Likewise, when a dominant bitch is bred to a dominant stud, the resulting litter is usually a failure; this explains why some "dream breedings" result in puppies that do not approach the quality of either parent.

Fig. 14. Reading a Pedigree

Sire: An upstanding black/tan dog with light markings, very good neck and shoulders, good pads and an excellent forechest...shoulders are laid back about 50 degrees...short-backed but a bit longer in the loin than desired...heavy coat has excellent texture.. good drape of stifle with short hocks and an outstanding head...have to look closely for tan markings... carries tail like a Terrier.

Ch. Hi-Boots Such Crust

Ch. Hi-Boots Such Brass

Dam: A square, black bitch standing about 13¾ inches with heavy bone and an excellent coat...lovely feminine head, but the neck is a bit short...back and loin are short...tail set is good and the rear quarters strong with low-set firm hocks...shoulders are well laid back with a good forechest.

Palmwood Portrait

Int. Ch. Maddie's Vagabond's Return

Fraternal Grandsire: A 15¼-inch buff dog with a reddish coat and silver furnishings...well laid-back shoulders with good forechest...strong, masculine head and neck that slopes nicely into clean shoulders...outline gives the appearance of being a bit long-backed...tail is set on level and carried level...strong hindquarters have well-muscled thighs and short hocks...coat could be more profuse.

Fraternal Grandam: A vividly (cream) marked black/tan, tall bitch going the full 14½ inches at the shoulder...beautiful shoulders that blend well into the body, and well-developed rib cage with the loin a bit on the long side...probably measures 13¼ inches down back to set on of tail...hindquarters well rounded with lots of muscle and a good bend of stifle with short, well let down hocks...plush head with vivid markings... average coat length with good texture.

Ch. DeKarlos Day Dreams

Ch. Cracker Box Certainly

Maternal Grandsire: A well-marked black/tan with correct neck and shoulders...lacks a bit in forechest...very good head lacking a bit of squareness of muzzle...very short back with proper length of loin...tail set on correctly but carried like a Terrier...well-rounded rear quarters with a bit more angulation than necessary...short, well let down hocks.

Ch. Palmwood Ace High Pattern

Maternal Grandam: A tall (14½") black bitch with good coat and lovely head...great neck and shoulders blending into a well-developed spring of rib...tendency to be somewhat long in loin...rear quarters well developed and set on correctly...hocks are short and well let down...overall impression is that of a rangy bitch with an outstanding head.

There are some dominant sires and dams that pass on their producing ability to their children, grandchildren, great-grandchildren, and so forth. Thus, some lines are noted for their outstanding producing ability. A producing dam, usually with a heritage of producing dams behind her, bred to a proven stud dog will usually come through with a top-quality litter.

What are the characteristics of a top-producing dam?

A stud dog's production is unlimited: a popular stud may sire hundreds and hundreds of puppies. Conversely, a bitch is strictly limited in the number of offspring she may produce. The average bitch will produce only 20 or 30 puppies in her lifetime. Taking this limitation into account, it becomes clear that those bitches who produce top-quality puppies are rare and special.

The producing dam may or may not contribute to her puppies the qualities that she herself possesses. However, all of her puppies will typically bear a resemblance to one another regardless of the sire. Whether closely line-bred or outcrossed, whether bred to a sire of note or to a comparative unknown, the consistency of quality and type will be apparent in the offspring.

There is no way to determine in advance those bitches destined to become "producers." However, it is most likely that they will come from a line noted for the producing ability of its bitches.

Occasionally, a bitch will come along with little or no producing heritage, yet she will be a standout in producing ability. It can only be assumed that such a bitch inherited a genetic make-up different from that of her immediate ancestors. There are known instances in which a bitch will produce only with one particular dog and not with others. In such cases, the desired results are achieved through an ideal blending, rather than by virtue of dominance.

The genetic influence of some dams is extremely negative. Such a bitch bred to a dominant sire will produce top-quality puppies only as a result of the stud's dominance.

The availability of a true top-producing dam is limited. Whereas many may breed to the outstanding sires, few have access to the top-producing dams. Their offspring can and should command top prices: demand always exceeds supply. Their bitch puppies are highly valued, for it is primarily through them that continuity is achieved.

The dog you select to stand at stud should possess certain attributes. First, he should be masculine in appearance and conform closely to the breed standard. A mistake commonly made by breeders is to breed to a stud dog that is overdone in some features to a bitch with deficiencies in these areas. For example, breeding an oversize dog to a small bitch in the hope of getting average-size puppies. Unfortunately, this is a futile effort because genetics doesn't work this way. Extremes should be avoided for they only complicate and confuse a breeding program.

What should I look for when selecting a stud dog?

It is important that the stud dog comes from an unbroken line of producers on both his sire's and dam's side. That is, at least his sire, grandsires, and great-grandsires should have produced 10 or more champions each. If his sire is still young, he may not yet have produced 10 champions. However, you may be able to tell by reading dog magazines and by viewing his offspring whether he will reach that goal. This unbroken "producing" line helps ensure that the prospective stud is likely to be dominant for his good traits.

Once you have decided on a stud dog, the next step is to contact his owners – generally at a dog show – and reserve a date for breeding. A down payment of 25 percent will usually convince them that your intentions are serious.

When selecting a stud to complement your bitch, it is important to take into consideration his qualities as well as the qualities of his parents. For example, suppose your bitch has a less-than-perfect head. In order to improve this feature in her offspring, you may wish to breed her to a stud with a beautiful head. However, it is also important that his parents had beautiful heads: then the stud can be considered dominant for this trait. If the sire does not have

How can I use line-breeding to improve my stock?

parents with beautiful heads, or if only one parent has a beautiful head, the dog is recessive for this characteristic, and his chances of reproducing it are diminished. Remember, also, that closely line-bred dogs and bitches have a much better chance of being dominant for their characteristics.

What is the law of filial regression, and how does it apply to dog breeding?

Genetic research done by Francis Galton in the 18th Century led to his law of filial regression, or "drag of the race," which concludes that races tend to revert to mediocrity. Galton reached his conclusions from statistical studies of people. He found that the adult children of very tall parents tended to be, while taller than the average of the population, not so tall as the mean height of their parents; and that the children of short parents tended to be shorter than average, but taller than the mean height of their parents. His statistics reveal the tendency of exaggeration of type in the parents to grow smaller or to disappear in the progeny.

A great-producing sire or dam produces a much higher average of good dogs among its progeny. When a great-producing sire and a great-producing dam are mated together, the average quality of the progeny is brought to its highest level. However, the law of filial regression practically guarantees that most of the offspring, while above average in quality when compared to all dogs of their breed, will be inferior to their outstanding parents. Only the occasional one will be superior to, or even equal to, its excellent parents.

Briefly, what are the main principles of breeding?

The above discussion can be condensed into the following four principles:
1. Breed only to a dog with a history of producing top-flight stock.
2. Stay close within the chosen bloodline.
3. Be sure the breeding stock you use has an unbroken producing line.
4. Do not breed to a current winner unless it meets the above standards.

CHAPTER SUMMARY:

The superior offspring of two excellent, top-producing dogs are likely to be top-producing.

An assortment of famous sires and dams in a dog's pedigree does not guarantee the quality of that dog's offspring. Each ancestor must also be a link in an unbroken chain of top producers.

The only tangible proof of a dog's ability to pass on superior traits is in the quality of the offspring.

The most effective combination of sire and dam is when one is dominant and the other is non-dominant.

An outstanding specimen that was produced as a result of line-breeding has a good chance of passing on desirable traits.

The law of filial regression states that exaggeration of type in the parents tends to diminish in the succeeding offspring.

14 Mating

"the breeder's art"

It's a godsend to find a prepotent stud with the breed characteristics you're seeking. Unfortunately for most of us, such a dog comes along once in a lifetime, if at all. If this is your experience, it is probably not wise to keep a male. After all, you can pick and choose and breed to the best in the country for an affordable stud fee. If you choose to keep a male, the likelihood of using him across all your bitches is great. Just as horsemen say "different horses for different courses," different bitches should be bred to dogs that suit them, both for pedigree and conformation.

If you do decide to keep a stud dog, be sure he has the qualities you want to have in the next generation. If he has a lovely head and his sire also had one, but his dam did not, then your chances of him being dominant for that good head are down the tubes. He is hetrozygous (non-dominant) for that trait when he should be homozygous (dominant) for it. Check on all his structural parts in the same way, and also be sure of the dispositions of his immediate ancestors.

Only keep a male if he satisfies all of the above criteria and pleases you as a balanced dog who is representative of his breed. DO NOT keep an oversized stallion because you think the breed needs the size, nor keep an extra "typey" little dog for the opposite reason. Intelligent breeders breed to what is right and shun extremes like the plague.

If you find the right one – read on and learn how to care for and promote him properly. AG

How should the young stud dog be socialized?

A young stud dog should be taught to get along with other male dogs. Avoid putting him with an older male too early on. If you do, there is a good likelihood that he'll be intimidated by the older male, and it may harm his prospects of being a good stud. Dogs who have been intimidated seldom learn to be aggressive during breeding, and end up failing in the breeding box. However, running, playing, and even puppy fighting with litter mates or slightly older puppies don't seem to have a detrimental effect.

Until the young male is old enough to defend himself, he should be quartered first with puppies his own age, and then with older bitches. It's not a good idea to keep him in a pen by himself because early socialization is extremely important. Time for play as a puppy, and a companion to keep him from boredom, helps his growth and development.

Why do a sperm count exam?

An important aspect of being the owner of a stud dog is to make sure he can produce puppies. Therefore, at around 11 or 12 months of age, it's a good idea to trundle him off to the veterinarian for a check on his sperm count. This will indicate if the dog is producing enough viable sperm cells to fertilize eggs in the ovum of a bitch. Sometimes, it's found that while a stud produces spermatozoa, they are not active. The chances of this dog being able to fertilize an egg is markedly reduced. While this problem is usually found in older dogs, it happens often enough in young animals to be of concern. Thus, it is important to have the sperm count exam done annually.

Why might a dog have undescended testicles?

The testicles and penis are the male organs of reproduction. The testicles are housed in a sac called the scrotum. The AKC will not allow dogs who are cryptorchids (neither testicle descended) or monorchids (only one testicle descended) to be shown for conformation points.

The scrotum acts as a thermostat. It contracts and expands in an effort to maintain the testes at the ideal temperature for sperm production. It may also contract when a dog is threatened with physical harm (for example, at the sight of a strange dog). The

Fig. 15. Left side of dog, showing genital organs

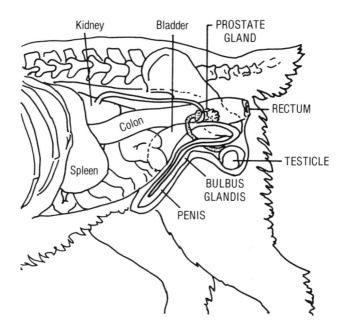

contraction does not force the testicles back up into the abdominal cavity of the adult dog because the inguinal rings have tightened and will not allow them through. This tightening of the rings usually occurs at about 10 months of age.

There are a number of reasons why a dog may have undescended testicles: the inguinal rings may be too small to allow the testicles to descend; the spermatic cord, the bundle of nerves, arteries, connective tissues, and ducts which nourish the testes, may be too short; or the testes may be trapped above the inguinal rings as the puppy matures.

When you place a male puppy on the grooming table to practice stacking, be careful when checking his testicles. The scrotal muscles may contract, and the still-generous inguinal rings may allow the testicles to ascend into the abdominal cavity permanently.

When do bitches first come into heat?

Many of the smaller and medium-sized breeds will come into their first heat between nine and thirteen months of age; larger breeds may wait as long as 18 months before their first heat. If your bitch is overdue for her first heat by more than five months, take her to your vet for a checkup.

Well-developed bitches of small and medium breeds, who are at least 10 months old, may be bred on their first season. However, it is usually wiser to wait six more months, until her second season. Also, it is best for her first breeding to be before she is three years old.

What are the phases of the bitch's estrous cycle?

Bitches of most breeds come into heat twice a year. However, the Basenji, as well as some of the larger breeds, come into heat only once a year.

The first sign that your bitch is coming into heat is a flow of light red blood from her vulva. The flow tends to become darker as her season progresses, and then lightens and tapers off at the end of her season. At the same time, her vulva will begin to take on a large, swollen appearance. Although the bitch will begin to attract males during this time, she will usually not display any behavioral changes, and she is usually not ready to breed. This initial stage is called the proestrus phase, and typically lasts six to nine days. Mark the first date of her bleeding on your calendar, and expect her next season to begin approximately six months later.

Next comes the estrus phase, during which the flow of blood is straw colored. During this phase, the bitch displays maximum sexual receptivity. She will begin to rub up against things, and thrust her tail to one side in a flagging motion. If there is a male around, she may back into him and thrust her vulva in his face. Of course, if you want to breed her, this is the time. During this phase, the vulva softens, which makes it easier for the male to penetrate and secure a tie. This phase usually lasts six to twelve days.

Typically, bitches are most fertile between the 12th and 15th day of their cycle (starting from the first day of bleeding). However, there are exceptions. Some may be fertile earlier or later in their cycles. Therefore, the first time your bitch comes into heat,

Fig. 16. Female reproductive organs. Drawings by Beatrice McLaughlin. Courtesy of Popular Dogs Magazine.

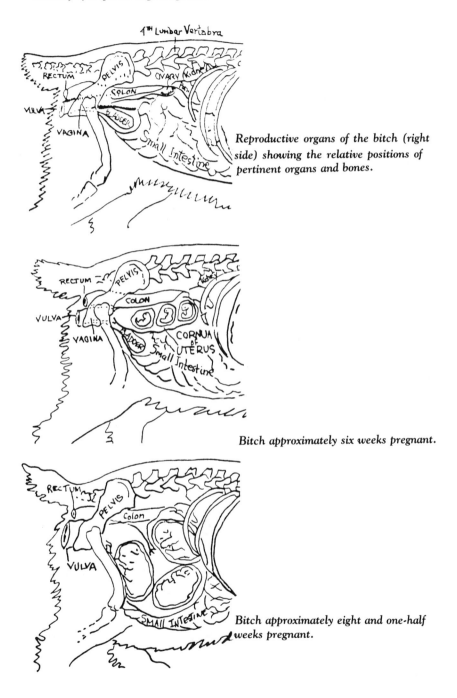

Reproductive organs of the bitch (right side) showing the relative positions of pertinent organs and bones.

Bitch approximately six weeks pregnant.

Bitch approximately eight and one-half weeks pregnant.

take her to the vet and have a smear done to determine when in her cycle she ovulates. After that, if you decide to breed her, you can use that expected date of ovulation to determine when to send her to the stud dog.

What can I do to prepare the bitch for breeding?

Take your bitch to the vet for a check-up two or three months before her next season. Have him check for: general condition; development; parasites, such as worms, ticks, and fleas; anemia; sexual diseases, such as brucellosis; and skin problems, such as eczema. Also, make sure all vaccinations are current. If health problems surface, there will be sufficient time to clear them up before her next season. It is especially important to rid her of parasites and contagious diseases, for these could be passed on to the puppies.

If your bitch is overweight, now is the time to put her on a diet: A fat dog has more difficulty conceiving and whelping. Conversely, if the bitch is underweight, pregnancy could deplete her already scant reserves. Her puppies might be weak and undernourished, and her milk supply may be inadequate to ensure their survival.

How can I prevent my dog from contracting a sexual disease?

Sexual contact with a variety of mates exposes dogs to infection. Some of these infections, if not promptly identified and treated, can lead to sterility. Other non-sexual infections and illnesses, such as urinary infections and kidney stones, can also reduce a dog's ability to produce puppies.

It's a good idea to have your vet check your bitch for brucellosis before and after each breeding. Brucellosis is passed by sexual contact and can cause sterility and abortions. Unfortunately, there is presently no vaccination or treatment for brucellosis. Therefore, prevention is of paramount importance. If you are the owner of the stud dog, you may wish to have your dog, as well as each bitch, checked for infection by your own vet before breeding. At the same time, your vet can also run a smear to see if the bitch is ready to breed.

The stud dog should be checked frequently to see if there is any discharge from the penis. A dog at regular stud should not have a discharge. After breeding, cleanse the stud dog's genital area with a sterile saline solution. Your vet may also advise flushing out the penile area with a special solution after breeding.

If you have chosen to breed your bitch to a dog who lives quite a distance away, you may need to fly the bitch to the stud dog. Before deciding on an airline, visit your local air freight office and speak with the agent in charge so that you can determine how the freight staff will handle your dog. Make sure that animals are promptly unloaded off all flights; that animals are not left on the tarmac for any great length of time; that the animals are given fresh water during long layovers and plane changes; and, that there are special procedures to care for animals during hot weather.

How do I transport my bitch to a distant stud?

As a general rule, the bitch is in the air such a short time that water is not a problem; you can lock a small water container onto the door of the crate. If the dog has to change planes, the ground crew will usually try to water the animal if the crate can remain closed. Also, it is a good idea to attach a sign to the crate that says, "Bitch In Season – Please Water but Don't Open Crate."

When your bitch is ready to breed, take her to the airport, properly crated, and stay at the airport until the plane has been loaded and taken off. At this time, call the dog's breeder and inform him that the bitch is on her way. It is the responsibility of the breeder to be at the destination airport on arrival. You'll want to confirm this because it could be quite unnerving to the bitch to have to wait in a strange place for a long period of time.

You won't need to send any special food with the bitch unless she is an extremely finicky eater.

Many foreign countries, as well as the state of Hawaii, have severe quarantine requirements which make breeding to dogs outside the area practically impossible. If the ideal mate for your dog is essentially unavailable due to quarantine restrictions or due to great distance, you may want to consider a breeding

What if the stud lives in another country, or in Hawaii?

through artificial insemination. For more information about this sophisticated method of dog breeding, check with your vet. You may also be able to gather information from dog publications, and from the AKC. (See Appendix for a list of sperm-gathering and storage sites.)

How should the stud dog be introduced to the bitch in heat?

When the bitch is ready to breed (as the stud gains experience he will not pay too much attention to her until she is ready) both animals should be allowed to exercise and relieve themselves just before being brought together. It's also a good idea not to feed them before mating. Bring the bitch in first. The breeding area should be quiet and away from noise and other dogs. Spend a few minutes petting her, speaking softly and kindly to her. Then, bring the stud dog in on a lead. Do not allow him to lunge in and leap at her. This can cause her to panic, and she may bite him out of fear.

After a few minutes of allowing the dogs to get acquainted, take the lead off the stud dog. Then let the two dogs court for a few more minutes. The bitch should let you know she is ready by continually backing into the dog.

How can I assist the dogs in achieving a successful "tie?"

Place the bitch on a large, non-skid rug, add a little Vaseline around the vulva, and face her rump toward the dog. Pat her on the fanny to encourage the dog to come ahead – usually he will. As a rule, he will lick her around the vulva. Some stud dogs will go around to the front and tenderly lick at the bitch's eyes and ears. If he does this, gently encourage him to come around to her rear. If he is unsure of himself, lift the bitch's rear and place it in front of his nose.

The male will mount the bitch from the rear and begin to probe slowly for the opening to the vagina. Once he discovers it, he will begin to move more rapidly. This is a critical time. A young dog can often be so far off target that he fails to get the distended penis near the vaginal opening. If this occurs, gently reposition the bitch so the male has a better angle. You may have to do this a number of times – don't worry, this ineptitude is normal in a young, inexperienced stud dog. The dog may even get frustrated and back off. Or, he may get so excited and confused that he swings around and tries to breed her from the front.

If the dog is becoming frustrated and having minimal success, take a break and separate the dogs for a couple of hours. It's important not to let the stud dog wear himself out – this lack of success can make him lose interest. Pet him and tell him how well he is doing. At the end of the rest break, try again. The approach should be the same. If after 20 minutes the stud is again unsuccessful, call it a day. The following day, you can try again, repeating the entire procedure.

By now you will have noticed a red, bone-like protuberance extending from the stud dog's penis sheath. This is the penis itself. When the dog has achieved penetration, the "bulbus glandis" just behind the pointed penis bone will begin to swell. The bulbous gland swells because it is filling with blood – it becomes about three times larger than the rest of the penis. In this way, the dog is "tied" to the bitch.

When a tie has occurred the semen is pumped in spurts into the vagina. Some ties last for up to an hour, some last only five minutes or so. A five-minute tie can be just as satisfactory as a longer one, because the semen can move up through the uterus and

What happens while the dogs are tied?

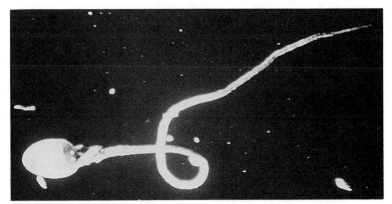

Male spermatazoa, showing whiplike propulsion

fallopian tubes to the ovarian capsules within five minutes.

Once the dog and bitch are successfully tied, the male will usually attempt to lift his rear leg over the bitch and keep the tie in a back-to-back position. However, some dogs merely slide off the bitch's back and maintain a tie facing in the same direction. One thing you can count on, though, the dogs will not stay in one position for any length of time. Because of this, it's a good idea to have two people helping: one at the bitch's head and the other at the male's.

What happens after the tie is broken?

After the tie has been broken, there sometimes will be a rush of fluid from the bitch's vulva. Don't worry about this; most of the sperm is already well on its way up the fallopian tubes. Gently move the bitch to a quiet pen, apart from the other dogs, and give her fresh water and an opportunity to relieve herself.

The stud dog should be petted and praised. This is also a good time to flush out his penile area; and if your vet has recommended any medication, apply this now. Then, the stud, too, should be placed in a separate, quiet pen with fresh water. It's a good idea to keep him away from other male dogs because the likelihood of a serious fight is high now: the other dogs would smell him and might become upset that it wasn't their turn.

How often should the bitch be serviced?

The individual bitch should be serviced twice by the stud dog – once every other day – for the best chance of conception.

How often can the dog be used at stud?

An experienced, well-conditioned dog can be used at stud once a day for up to seven days in a row, or twice a day for up to three days. However, if a dog is seldom used, he should not be expected to perform day-after-day for any great length of time. An abundance of activity may be possible for a short time, but three times a week seems to be the optimal amount for good health and good management of the stud dog. Generally, a dog may stand at stud until he is about 10 years old.

If the bitch is in good condition, she may be bred two seasons in a row, especially if her season has been delayed because of having a litter. However, it is usually wiser to skip every other season. Having a litter can exhaust the bitch's calcium supply and reproductive system; she needs time to recover before being bred again. Generally, bitches may produce litters until they are about eight years old. Statistics indicate that greatest puppy mortality occurs in first litters. Survival is higher during the second through fifth litters, and then mortality increases again after the fifth litter.

How often may a bitch conceive a litter of puppies?

CHAPTER SUMMARY:

The stud dog needs to gain self-confidence at an early age, so that he will be confident and aggressive in the breeding box.

A sperm-count exam should be performed annually on the stud dog. Stud dogs with one or both testicles undescended may be bred, if they are fertile. They may also compete at field trials and obedience trials, but they may not compete for conformation points.

Bitches usually come into their first heat between nine and eighteen months of age, and usually come into heat twice a year.

It is usually best to wait for the bitch's second season before breeding her, and for the first breeding to take place before she is three years old.

Bitches are usually most fertile between the 12th and 15th day of their season.

Prior to breeding your bitch, arrange to have her thoroughly examined by your vet at least two or three months before her next season.

Have your bitch checked by your vet for sexual diseases before and after each breeding.

As the owner of a stud dog, have each incoming bitch

checked for sexual diseases by your vet before breeding. Also, check often for discharge from the dog's penis.

Before shipping your bitch off to the stud dog, make sure the airline will take proper care of her from the beginning of the flight to the destination.

If the stud dog lives quite a distance away, or is unavailable because of restrictive quarantine laws, you may want to consider a breeding through artificial insemination.

Bring the bitch into the breeding area first, then bring in the male on a lead.

Keep the dog interested in the bitch's rear, and don't allow him to dissipate his energy.

If the dog is having difficulty achieving penetration, separate him from the bitch for a couple of hours.

Following successful penetration, the dogs may be "tied" for up to 20 minutes; during this time they will be moving around a bit. To prevent the tie from being broken prematurely, position one person at the male's head and one at the bitch's.

After the tie is broken, remove the bitch and the dog to separate, quiet pens, away from each other and from any other dogs.

The bitch should be serviced twice, once every other day.

A dog can be used at stud about three times a week, on average, until he is about 10 years old.

Generally, it is wisest to breed your bitch no more often than every other season.

Puppy survival is highest in the second through fifth litters.

PART IV
RAISING THE LITTER

15 Whelping

"midwifery at its best"

Here they come, ready or not. Sixty-three days passes very fast, so you need to use your time wisely to prepare for the big event.

Sixty-three days – give or take a few days – make the anticipation all the more fun. Let's be truthful, almost anything is possible, although the majority of whelpings go well. Just be prepared. Talking to your vet ahead of time and letting him know the whelping date so he'll be available is certainly a wise thing to do. I also suggest purchasing the video, *Puppies, Puppies – Here They Come, Ready or Not* (Doral Publishing, Inc.). You can, at the least, laugh at the trials and tribulations of a typical couple whelping their first litter.

Proper whelping and raising of a litter can make all the difference in the world in the show-ring attitudes of the puppies. A calm, loving mother and patient, soothing socialization of the babies can go a long way toward getting them off on the right foot. AG

For the first three weeks of pregnancy, the bitch requires no special care. As usual, she should have good nourishment, fresh water, and regular exercise. If she was not wormed before breeding, check with the vet to see if she needs it now. However, be sure your vet knows she is pregnant before she is wormed: worming can be dangerous to the fetuses.

From the fourth through the sixth week, gradually increase her intake to twice the normal, and feed her

Does the pregnant bitch require special care?

twice a day to aid digestion. Eliminate jumping, running, and rough play with other dogs; walking is now the best exercise for her.

Starting with the seventh week, eliminate any hard-to-digest foods, and spread her feedings out to three times a day. Be sure to continue walking her briskly on lead, but be careful not to let her overextend herself physically.

The week before she is due to whelp, modify her diet by making it more liquid; this will assist her elimination.

Within three days of whelping, give her a teaspoonful of milk of magnesia daily to help clear out her intestinal tract before delivery.

How can I prepare the bitch for whelping?

Beginning about one week before the bitch is due, clean her teeth daily using a mixture of table salt and baking soda. This tends to lessen the possibility of navel and other infections in the newborn puppies.

Next, bathe her thoroughly with a mild soap, such as Dove, paying special attention to cleaning her breasts and abdomen. If she has an extremely heavy coat, the hair around the breasts should be massaged with baby oil to loosen any accumulated crusts. Also, cut short any long hair on the insides and backs of her hind legs, and clip her tail hair short; this will help keep the whelping less messy, and may also prevent a puppy from becoming tangled in it. You probably will not need to clip the hair around her breasts; it usually starts to fall off of its own accord about two weeks before whelping, in preparation for nursing. If you wish, you may help the process by gently combing the hair away from the breast area.

Skin problems, such as eczema, are usually worsened by the stress of nursing. Parasites, such as lice, fleas, and ticks, may also be much more bothersome to the bitch when she is nursing, and may also infest the newborn puppies. Therefore, make every effort to rid the bitch of these problems before whelping. Be sure, though, not to leave insecticides on the bitch's skin late in the pregnancy. Instead, bathe her in flea and tick shampoo, and rinse thoroughly.

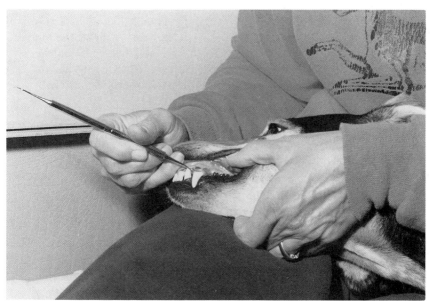

Cleaning teeth

The average pregnancy is 63 days, counting from the day of breeding. (If she was bred twice, count from the day of the first breeding.) However, no two pregnancies are alike, and whelping can occur anytime between the 59th and the 65th day.

Refer to the Sixty-Three Day Whelping Table, to calculate the date your bitch is due.

How long is the average pregnancy?

The whelping box should be prepared at least two weeks before the due date. Encourage the bitch to sleep in the whelping box at night and at naptime so that she becomes used to it. Make sure that the area you choose for whelping is quiet and comfortable, and that there will not be a parade of visitors – people or dogs during whelping.

The dimensions of the whelping box depend on the size of the breed. For instance, a medium-sized breed, such as a Cocker Spaniel, would need a box that measured approximately four feet square. The box should have enough room for the bitch to whelp the puppies without feeling crowded, and should also allow you room to assist with whelping, if necessary.

How do I construct a whelping box?

The sides of the box need to be high enough to keep the puppies in and cold drafts out – about two feet high for a medium-sized breed. A lip at the top of the wall, facing in, can also help prevent the growing puppies from escaping. In addition, the box should sit at least two inches above the floor to help insulate the puppies from drafts.

Build a 12-inch high partition inside the box to allow the dam a place where she can occasionally "escape" from the puppies. Around the inside of the box, construct a railing two or three inches above the floor and two or three inches out from the walls. Puppies who sleep at the side of the whelping box will be underneath the rail; this will prevent them from being inadvertently trapped and crushed beneath their mother.

The floor of the whelping box should be covered with a rough surface, like indoor/outdoor carpeting, to provide the puppies with some traction while they are nursing. Before the bitch whelps, cover the carpeting with shredded newspaper. This allows the bitch in labor to dig as she tries to nest; and it also helps keep the whelping area sanitary, since newspaper is antiseptic. After the puppies are two weeks old the dam will probably stop cleaning up after them, so then cover the carpeting with layers of newspaper (unshredded). Be sure to replace soiled newspaper often, to keep the whelping box clean.

For about the first 10 days of life, newborn puppies are unable to generate enough body heat to survive; they have no shivering mechanism. Therefore, it's imperative to supply heat externally. Place a heating source either under the floor of the whelping box or just above the box, to guard the puppies against hypothermia. For example, you may want to string a high-wattage light bulb above the box. The air temperature in the box needs to be 85° to 90° Fahrenheit during the first 10 days of life. Set up the heating source before the puppies are born, and check the temperature to make sure it's warm enough, but not too warm.

Because puppies usually don't come all at once, a place is needed to keep the newborns in sight of the mother, but out of the way as she whelps the next one. You can use a small, clean cardboard box with high sides for this purpose. Place a heating pad or hot water bottle in the bottom of the box and cover it with a towel. You will need to monitor the heating pad at all times; the towel should feel warm, not hot, to the touch. You may also need a second cardboard box, complete with hot-water bottle and towel, to take along on a trip to the vet's, if this becomes necessary.

Clean, sharp scissors and clean, light-weight string should be nearby, placed in a container filled with isopropyl (rubbing) alcohol. These may be used to cut the umbilical cord and tie it off, if necessary. Also, have available a shallow dish of iodine in which to dip the end of the umbilical cord.

A rubber, bulb syringe may be needed to clear a puppy's nose and lungs of excess fluid. These are commonly available at drugstores and in the "baby" section of grocery stores. They are sometimes labelled "aspirators" or "nasal aspirators." You should also have on hand a small container of brandy or whiskey, along with an eyedropper: these may be needed to stimulate a lethargic puppy.

Disposable towels, washcloths, cotton swabs, a garbage pail, mild soap, and several pans for warm and cold water should be close at hand to help keep the whelping area, puppies, bitch, and you antiseptic. The pans may also be needed to help stimulate a lethargic puppy.

Last, have on hand a notebook, pencil, clock, and scale in order to record the time of birth and weight or each puppy.

What supplies should I have on hand for the delivery?

As the time to whelp approaches, most bitches will exhibit many of the following signs: shivering, panting, restlessness, refusal to eat, digging, staring, and vaginal discharge. However, the most accurate predictor of the event is rectal temperature. Take the bitch's temperature twice a day, starting on the 59th day of gestation. A dog's normal temperature is 101° F. to 102° F. When her temperature drops below 99°

What are the signs of imminent labor?

Fig. 17. 63-Day Whelping Table

Date Bred	Puppies Due	Date Bred	Puppies Due	Date Bred	Puppies Due	Date Bred	Puppies Due	Date Bred	Puppies Due	Date Bred	Puppies Due	Date Bred	Puppies Due	Date Bred	Puppies Due	Date Bred	Puppies Due	Date Bred	Puppies Due	Date Bred	Puppies Due	Date Bred	Puppies Due
JANUARY	MARCH	FEBRUARY	APRIL	MARCH	MAY	APRIL	JUNE	MAY	JULY	JUNE	AUGUST	JULY	SEPTEMBER	AUGUST	OCTOBER	SEPTEMBER	NOVEMBER	OCTOBER	DECEMBER	NOVEMBER	JANUARY	DECEMBER	FEBRUARY
1	5	1	5	1	3	1	3	1	3	1	3	1	2	1	3	1	3	1	3	1	3	1	2
2	6	2	6	2	4	2	4	2	4	2	4	2	3	2	4	2	4	2	4	2	4	2	3
3	7	3	7	3	5	3	5	3	5	3	5	3	4	3	5	3	5	3	5	3	5	3	4
4	8	4	8	4	6	4	6	4	6	4	6	4	5	4	6	4	6	4	6	4	6	4	5
5	9	5	9	5	7	5	7	5	7	5	7	5	6	5	7	5	7	5	7	5	7	5	6
6	10	6	10	6	8	6	8	6	8	6	8	6	7	6	8	6	8	6	8	6	8	6	7
7	11	7	11	7	9	7	9	7	9	7	9	7	8	7	9	7	9	7	9	7	9	7	8
8	12	8	12	8	10	8	10	8	10	8	10	8	9	8	10	8	10	8	10	8	10	8	9
9	13	9	13	9	11	9	11	9	11	9	11	9	10	9	11	9	11	9	11	9	11	9	10
10	14	10	14	10	12	10	12	10	12	10	12	10	11	10	12	10	12	10	12	10	12	10	11
11	15	11	15	11	13	11	13	11	13	11	13	11	12	11	13	11	13	11	13	11	13	11	12
12	16	12	16	12	14	12	14	12	14	12	14	12	13	12	14	12	14	12	14	12	14	12	13
13	17	13	17	13	15	13	15	13	15	13	15	13	14	13	15	13	15	13	15	13	15	13	14
14	18	14	18	14	16	14	16	14	16	14	16	14	15	14	16	14	16	14	16	14	16	14	15
15	19	15	19	15	17	15	17	15	17	15	17	15	16	15	17	15	17	15	17	15	17	15	16
16	20	16	20	16	18	16	18	16	18	16	18	16	17	16	18	16	18	16	18	16	18	16	17
17	21	17	21	17	19	17	19	17	19	17	19	17	18	17	19	17	19	17	19	17	19	17	18
18	22	18	22	18	20	18	20	18	20	18	20	18	19	18	20	18	20	18	20	18	20	18	19
19	23	19	23	19	21	19	21	19	21	19	21	19	20	19	21	19	21	19	21	19	21	19	20
20	24	20	24	20	22	20	22	20	22	20	22	20	21	20	22	20	22	20	22	20	22	20	21
21	25	21	25	21	23	21	23	21	23	21	23	21	22	21	23	21	23	21	23	21	23	21	22
22	26	22	26	22	24	22	24	22	24	22	24	22	23	22	24	22	24	22	24	22	24	22	23
23	27	23	27	23	25	23	25	23	25	23	25	23	24	23	25	23	25	23	25	23	25	23	24
24	28	24	28	24	26	24	26	24	26	24	26	24	25	24	26	24	26	24	26	24	26	24	25
25	29	25	29	25	27	25	27	25	27	25	27	25	26	25	27	25	27	25	27	25	27	25	26
26	30	26	30 May	26	28	26	28	26	28	26	28	26	27	26	28	26	28	26	28	26	28	26	27
27	31 Apr	27	1	27	29	27	29	27	29	27	29	27	28	27	29	27	29	27	29	27	29	27	28 Mar
28	1	28	2	28	30	28	30 Jul	28	30	28	30	28	29	28	30	28	30 Dec	28	30	28	30	28	1
29	2			29	31	29	1	29	31	29	31	29	30	29	31	29	1	29	31	29	31	29	2
30	3			30	1 Jun	30	2	30	1 Aug	30	1 Sep	30	1 Oct	30	1 Nov	30	2	30	1 Jan	30	1 Feb	30	3
31	4			31	2			31	2			31	2	31	2			31	2			31	4

F., whelping will probably begin within 12 hours. Then, alert your vet to stand by in case any problems arise. If your vet is unavailable, you'll want to make specific arrangements for another practitioner.

Assuming that the bitch's temperature has dropped and she is exhibiting several of the signs mentioned above, the breaking of the amniotic sac (sometimes called the "breaking of the water") signals the onset of true labor. The amount of amniotic fluid varies – it may be scanty or profuse. Sometimes this event is very obvious: suddenly the bitch may appear to be sitting in a puddle of water. Other times the breaking of the amniotic sac may not be obvious, especially if the bitch is restless, digging up her papers, and constantly moving around. Still other times, the amniotic sac may extend from the vulva like a balloon. When this happens, do not interfere with it; allow it to break of its own accord. After the sac has broken, the first puppy should arrive any time from a few minutes to half an hour later. There is usually a show of fluid before the arrival of each puppy.

Fig. 18. Checklist of Items Needed for Whelping

1. *small, clean cardboard box*
2. *heating pad*
3. *hot water bottle*
4. *lightweight string for tying off umbilical cord*
5. *towels for drying off puppies*
6. *clean, sharp scissors*
7. *bulb syringe*
8. *rubbing alcohol*
9. *lots of clean newspapers*
10. *vet's phone number*
11. *contact vet ahead of time so he can be on call*
12. *small amount of brandy*
13. *eyedropper*
14. *cotton swabs*
15. *garbage pail*
16. *mild soap*
17. *several pans for warm and cold water*
18. *pencil/pen*
19. *paper for recording birth times, weight, sex, and color of puppies*
20. *scale*
21. *iodine for touching up ends of umbilical cord*
22. *at vet's recommendation, and with experience only, vet-prescribed medication to speed up sluggish delivery*
23. *syringe with sharp disposable needle*

In a normal delivery, the bitch will begin straining soon after the water breaks. Straining is an obvious muscular contraction, is fairly slow and steady, and is characterized by an arched back and raised tail – the bitch is obviously laboring to expel the puppy. The bitch may strain once and then rest for a few minutes. With the next contraction, she may strain two or three times in a row. Usually, by the time she strains five or six times in succession, the puppy is about to be whelped. The bitch may give birth either lying down or squatting.

When the puppy arrives, the normal presentation is head first. The head of the newborn puppy is the largest portion of its body; when the head arrives first, the remainder of the puppy slips out easily. A puppy sometimes arrives quickly and forcefully, and is deposited unceremoniously on the floor of the whelping box. At other times, a bubble appears to emerge from the bitch, becoming larger each time she strains. The puppy will emerge entirely enclosed in the sac, dangling between the bitch's hind legs. If this happens, grasp the umbilical cord close to the bitch and pull firmly but gently. This should also dislodge the placenta from within the bitch.

Usually, the bitch will reach back, break the sac, and cut the puppy's umbilical cord with her teeth. Then she will start to lick the puppy. After she has cleaned it she may wish to nurse. However, most of the time, she will begin to prepare for her next whelp. If she digs at the shredded papers, remove the newborn puppy and place it in the separate, warmed cardboard box. You may wish to leave the cardboard box in the corner of the whelping box. However, if the bitch starts to whirl around, remove the box to a safer location. Just be sure the mother can see the box at all times – otherwise, she may become agitated.

Typically, puppies are born at intervals of 10 to 30 minutes, but sometimes there can be one or two hours between deliveries. As long as the bitch does not seem distressed, any pattern can be considered normal. However, if for any reason you are worried that the whelping is not progressing normally, call your vet for advice.

If a puppy is not whelped after 20 minutes of straining, something is usually wrong. It could be that the puppy is being presented breech or sideways, or is abnormally large. In either case, call your vet: Your bitch needs help whelping the puppies.

If you need to take your bitch in to the vet, bring an assistant along with you to help deliver puppies in the car, if it becomes necessary. Also, bring that other small box with a hot water bottle in it, covered with a towel, to keep warm any puppies born at the vet's office.

What if the bitch seems distressed?

As soon as the puppy emerges completely, the sac must be broken immediately, and the umbilical cord severed. If the bitch does not do so at once, or if she seems confused, you will need to help her. This is most likely to happen with the bitch's first litter. However, sometimes even an experienced dam may bite the cord off too close to the puppy's navel – this can cause bleeding and infection, possibly even a hernia. Again, you may need to assist the bitch with the task of cleaning up the puppies and severing the umbilical cords.

Help the bitch break the puppy's sac and encourage her to lick the puppy. If she will not, then gently, but firmly, rub the puppy with a dry, clean towel: this will clean the puppy, as well as stimulate a cry. Be sure to hold the puppy's head downwards to help drain excess fluid from the lungs.

Next, hold the puppy lower than the placenta, and cut the cord one or two inches from the puppy. The puppy's end of the cord can be dipped in iodine and then tied off with a small piece of light-weight string, taken from the container of rubbing alcohol. The ends of the string should be cut short so that the dam can't pull on them and damage the puppy's navel. After the puppy has been rubbed somewhat dry, give it back to the bitch to lick and admire.

When and how should I cut the umbilical cord?

It is not uncommon for the new arrival to greet the world feet first in a breech presentation. When the head arrives last, it has a more difficult time passing through the opening. This can make whelping a little more difficult, but usually doesn't cause major problems.

How can I assist with a breech presentation?

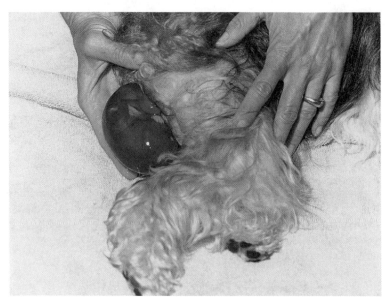

Puppy coming out head first

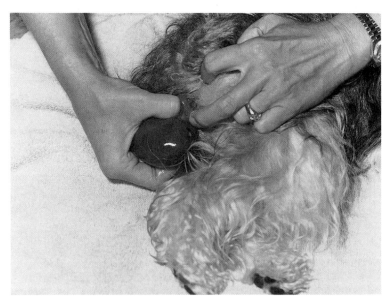

Assisting by pulling the puppy out

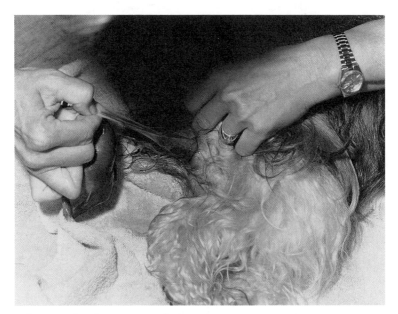

Pulling out the placentas attached to sac

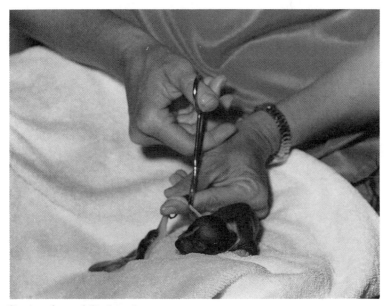

Cutting the umbilical cord

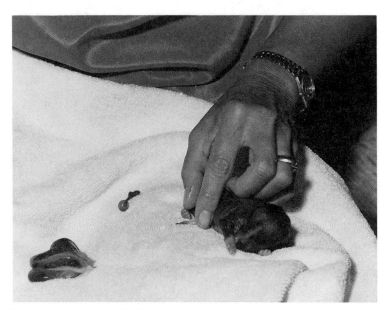

Showing cut cord and afterbirth

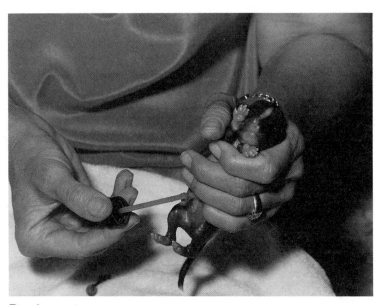

Disinfecting the cut cord

When the puppy arrives feet first, its feet may protrude and dangle from the vulva. If the rest of the body does not follow immediately, grasp the hindquarters of the puppy with a clean towel. With gentle pressure, slowly rotate the body and pull gently as the bitch strains. Breech birth can sometimes be aided by elevating the bitch's front legs slightly and gently massaging her abdomen from front to rear. If you are not able to dislodge the puppy, and it keeps slipping back into the bitch, get her to the vet.

Sometimes a puppy is whelped that appears lifeless or lethargic. First try to stimulate the puppy by vigorous but gentle rubbing. If this fails, immerse the puppy – except for the head, of course in cold water, and then in quite warm water. Keep alternating cold with warm until the shock stimulates the puppy to gasp and squeal. A drop or two of brandy or whiskey placed on the puppy's tongue may also help.

What should I do if the puppy appears lifeless or wheezy?

If the puppy sounds wheezy or bubbly, it may have swallowed some of the fluid from the amniotic sac. This fluid must be expelled or it can cause artificial pneumonia in the puppy. Grasp the puppy firmly in both hands and swing it up, head first, over your head and then down between your knees. Repeated, gentle swinging will help expel the fluid. An infant nasal aspirator can also be used to suck excess fluid from the nose and mouth.

The puppy usually emerges from the dam enclosed in a sac. Generally, this sac is intact, but sometimes it is broken in the process of whelping. Most of the time, the placenta, or afterbirth, is attached to the sac. The placenta is a blackish mass almost as large as the puppy.

Why must I account for the placentas?

However, sometimes the placenta is not expelled along with the puppy, and a retained placenta can cause a serious uterine infection in the bitch. Therefore, it is vital to check for a placenta after each puppy is whelped. If the placenta does not follow immediately after the whelping of the puppy, it might appear just before the whelping of the next puppy or the one after that.

As each puppy is whelped, note on paper the time

of arrival, the sex, weight, and whether or not there was an placenta. This will avoid confusion should one or more of the placentas be delayed. Actually, you may want to have an assistant to help with the recordkeeping all during the dam's birthing process.

Many dams will eat the placenta; doing so stimulates delivery of the next puppies. However, if she makes no move to do so, remove and dispose of it. Let her eat the first two or three placentas, if she wishes, but eating more than that will probably give her diarrhea.

When you take the bitch in for her post-partum checkup, your vet will check to see if she has any retained placentas or puppies. If so, a shot of pituitrin, or a similar drug, may be given to induce contractions. This should help expel the retained matter.

What if labor is prolonged?

If there are indications of a long, drawn-out whelping, you may want to ask your vet about administering a pituitrin shot to the bitch (For example, if two hours elapse since the birth of the last puppy and you think there are more to be born). In appropriate circumstances, this shot will speed up the labor process considerably. Sluggish labor is usually due to lack of muscle tone in older bitches and in bitches who are out of shape. Sometimes a short walk around the room or in the yard (on leash!) will stimulate labor. Allowing an earlier arrival to nurse – if the bitch is willing – will sometimes stimulate labor.

Occasionally, a bitch may be unable to push the puppies down into the birth canal. In this event, your vet may decide to take these puppies surgically by Caesarean section. If your bitch needs a C-section, be sure to ask your vet for detailed instructions on how to care for her after she returns home.

What should I do after all the puppies are whelped?

After all the puppies have arrived, it is important for the bitch to go outside and relieve herself. If she is reluctant to leave the newborns, you will need to force her gently to go outside. Speak encouragingly, and be sure to stay with her in case another puppy is whelped unexpectedly.

Puppy after the sac is broken, showing placenta still attached

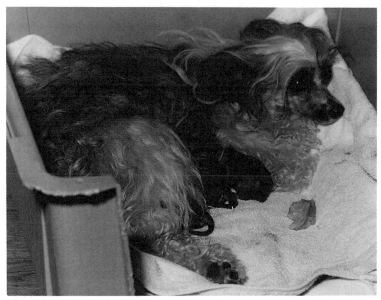

Nursing puppies

Next, sponge off the bitch's underside and clean her. Bitches are usually hungry after whelping, so offer her some milk and a bowl of her regular food. Then, clear away all the messy papers and put fresh, clean bedding in the whelping box – use rough toweling to provide traction for the puppies to nurse. Naturally, keep the bedding area clean at all times.

Place each puppy on a nipple and make sure they all suckle. This usually will come naturally to normal, robust puppies. Others might have to be shown how to nurse – place the dam's nipple in the puppy's mouth, making sure the tongue is under the nipple. You can also squeeze a few drops of milk onto the newborn's tongue.

It is of utmost importance that the puppies all suckle within a few hours after birth. This is because the first milk produced by the dam contains a special substance called colostrum. Ingestion of colostrum provides a natural immunity to many viral and bacterial diseases; this, in turn, provides the puppies a natural vaccination.

Healthy, contented puppies are quiet. When puppies cry or whine continually, something is wrong. First, check to be sure that the puppies are warm and out of any cold drafts. If the whining continues, you may want to call your vet.

Also, if the bitch will not settle down and you know for sure that all the puppies have been whelped, consult your vet; the dam may require a calcium shot to ward off a pre-eclampsia-type condition.

After whelping, the bitch should have a clear, red discharge from her vagina. This discharge should last about two weeks, and will diminish gradually. If the discharge is blackish or greenish in color, take her to your vet as soon as possible; she may need a shot of pituitrin to expel a retained placenta or puppy. If she has a uterine infection, an antibiotic may be prescribed.

CHAPTER SUMMARY:

The pregnant bitch should be walked regularly, and her regular diet should be doubled gradually over the course of the pregnancy.

Prepare the bitch for whelping by clearing up any skin problems, bathing her, and, if necessary, clipping the long hair from her hind quarters.

The average pregnancy is 63 days, counting from the day of the first breeding.

Prepare the whelping box two weeks before the bitch's due date, and help her get used to it by encouraging her to sleep in it.

Be sure that the air temperature of the whelping area is maintained at 85° to 90° F.

Collect all the items needed for whelping, and have everything available and organized in the whelping area at least one week before the due date.

A drop in the bitch's temperature – to below 99° F. is a sure sign that whelping will occur within 12 hours. Puppies are usually born at intervals of 10 to 30 minutes.

Be ready to help the bitch with cleaning the puppies and cutting the umbilical cords, especially if this is her first litter. Also be ready to help out with lethargic or wheezy puppies.

If, for any reason, you are worried that the whelping is not progressing normally, call your vet for advice.

A retained placenta can cause a serious uterine infection in the bitch: be sure that one complete placenta is expelled with each puppy.

After all the puppies are whelped, take the bitch outside to relieve herself. Then clean the bitch and the whelping box, and offer her some food and water. Next, place each newborn puppy on a nipple.

Taking Care of Newborn Puppies

"a major responsibility"

Taking proper care of your puppies is probably the most important thing you can do to develop winners early on. Even before socialization by humans begins, the physical care you give your puppies will pay off handsomely in healthy, sturdy puppies who can take advantage of their heredity.

It's amazing how well healthy puppies can come through the trauma of birth and the exposure to all the ailments of the alien world around them. Remember, they are helpless and depend entirely on their mother and on you for the first five weeks of their lives.

The information in this chapter and the one that follows could very well save a puppy's life – and yours, as a breeder. Read with great care and take heed. AG

Puppies should nurse for four to six weeks before being weaned. During that time, make sure that all the puppies are able to nurse. Sometimes, especially in a large litter, the smaller puppies don't get their fair share of milk. You may need to let the smaller puppies nurse twice a day, while the other puppies are kept away.

For how many weeks should a puppy nurse?

With a large litter, the dam may not have enough milk to provide adequate nutrition for all her puppies. In this case, or if the puppies are orphaned, premature, or weak, you will need to supplement her breast milk for the first three or four weeks of life. Some breeders supplement each litter as a matter of

When and how do I supplement the dam's milk?

course; they feel that it helps the weaning process as well as the growth and development of the puppies.

Several excellent milk substitutes are available at pet stores. You can also use goat's milk, which almost all puppies seem to relish. A third option is to prepare a home brew by mixing one can (13 ounces) of evaporated milk; one-third cup of water; two egg yolks; a few drops of human infant vitamins or one drop of oral vitamins for dogs; and two tablespoons of cream. Prepare just enough milk substitute for use within 48 hours, and be sure to keep the mixture refrigerated.

Under normal circumstances, feed the puppies three or four times each day, equally spaced. However, if the puppies are weak or small, it may be necessary to feed them up to six times daily. When it's time for a feeding, blend the milk substitute thoroughly and warm it to between 95° and 100° F. You can test for the proper temperature by squirting a few drops of milk onto the underside of your wrist. If the milk feels neither warm nor cold on your wrist, it's the perfect temperature. Once the puppies are seven to ten days old, however, you need only warm the milk substitute to room temperature before serving.

There are four methods commonly used to feed puppies: spoon-feeding, dropper-feeding, bottle-feeding, and tube-feeding. Spoon-feeding and dropper-feeding are difficult, inaccurate, time consuming, and dangerous. They entail pouring or dropping food into the puppy's mouth. The puppy's head must not be elevated or the food may enter his lungs and cause pneumonia. Dropper-feeding is usually a little faster and tidier than spoon-feeding, but it is still difficult to know how much food the puppy is actually consuming. The greatest danger of these two methods is not the difficulty of calculating the amount of food consumed, but, rather, it is the potential for choking the puppy and infecting his lungs. Experienced breeders almost always prefer bottle-feeding or tube-feeding.

Bottle-feeding is slow but rewarding. Use a doll-sized nipple for puppies of small breeds and for premature puppies. Most other puppies will take milk best from an orphan lamb nipple or a premature human baby nipple. If necessary, you can enlarge the hole in the nipple slightly with a hot needle. However, do not enlarge it too much; puppies will not nurse if the milk flows too rapidly. Before each feeding, squirt a little water through the nipple to make sure it isn't clogged. While feeding, be sure to hold the bottle so the puppy is less likely to swallow air.

Tube-feeding involves inserting a plastic tube into the puppy's stomach, and then releasing the formula from a syringe, through the tube and into the stomach. This is the easiest, cleanest, most accurate method of hand-feeding puppies. Indeed, it may be the best way of feeding a premature or weak puppy without the ability to suckle well. If you decide to tube-feed the puppies, be sure to have your vet or a fellow breeder demonstrate the method to you.

The most common problem associated with tube-feeding is overfeeding, which may, in turn, cause diarrhea. Be sure to calculate the daily caloric needs of your puppies, and to feed them the proper amount.

Fig. 19. Daily Caloric Needs of Puppies

Weeks	1	2	3	4	5	10	15	20	25	30	40	50	60	70
5	100	200	300	400	500	1000	1500							
6	90	180	270	360	450	900	1350							
7	80	160	240	320	400	800	1200							
8	75	150	225	300	375	750	1125	1500						
9	70	140	210	280	350	700	1050	1400						
10		130	195	260	325	650	975	1300	1625					
11			180	240	300	600	900	1200	1500					
12				224	280	560	840	1128	1400	1680				
13				208	260	520	780	1040	1300	1560				
14					240	480	720	960	1200	1440	1920			
15						450	675	900	1125	1350	1800			
16						420	630	840	1050	1260	1680	2100		
17							585	780	975	1170	1560	1950		
18								720	900	1080	1440	1800	2160	
19									825	990	1320	1650	1980	
										900	1280	1500	1800	2100

To determine the number of calories needed by a particular puppy, find the dog's weight in the top row of numbers and move downward until you come to the line corresponding to the dog's age. The figure in the spot where the two lines intersect is the number of calories that puppy needs during a 24-hour period.

The chart above represents average amounts. A puppy's individual needs may vary by as much as 25 percent above or below this average.

To calculate the caloric needs of a puppy, first weigh him on a sensitive, accurate scale. Next, multiply the calories needed per ounce (see above table) by the puppy's weight. For example, you may calculate the caloric needs of a three-day-old, 10-ounce puppy as follows:

4 calories/ounce/day x 10 ounces = 40 calories/day

This puppy needs 40 calories each day

If the milk substitute you're using contains 30 calories per ounce, you can calculate the number of ounces the puppy will need each day by dividing the number of calories needed each day by the calories in each ounce of milk substitute:

40 calories/day ÷ by 30 calories/ounce = 1.3 ounces/day

This puppy needs to consume 1.3 ounces of milk substitute each day

Next, divide the ounces of milk substitute needed each day by 3 to calculate the amount of milk substitute to give the puppy at each feeding:

1.3 ounces/milk substitute ÷ by 3 feedings/day = .43 ounces of milk substitute per feeding

Thus, a 10-ounce, three-day-old puppy needs just a little less than half an ounce of milk substitute three times a day.

How do I take care of orphaned puppies?

If the dam cannot or will not take care of her puppies, you will need to feed them, keep them clean, and make sure they do not become chilled or dehydrated. Newborn puppies cannot urinate or eliminate without assistance. Generally, the dam will lick their genital and anal areas to stimulate elimination. However, if the puppies are orphaned, you will need to perform this service. After each feeding, dip a swab, cottonball, or small piece of cloth in baby oil, and then rub it over the puppy's genital and anal areas – this should stimulate elimination. You will need to do this for about two weeks, until the puppies are functioning on their own.

Chilling is the leading cause of death in newborn

puppies. If the puppies are orphaned, steps must be taken to prevent chilling. You can place the puppies in an incubator, or use lukewarm heating pads, hot water bottles, or heat lamps to keep them warm. During the first four days of life, the environment should be 85° to 90° F.; it may then be gradually reduced to 80° F. by the 10th day; and then reduced again to 72° F. at the end of the fourth week.

Normal rectal temperature for a newborn puppy is 95° to 99° F. during the first week of life and 97° to 100° F. during the second and third weeks. By the fourth week, the puppy's temperature should reach 100.5° to 102.5° F., which is the normal temperature for an adult dog. If the puppy's rectal temperature drops below 94° F. at any time, take immediate action to warm the puppy slowly back up to normal temperature – remember that warming too rapidly can kill a puppy.

What are the causes and symptoms of dehydration?

Dehydration in newborn puppies is also a significant cause of puppy death. Dehydration can be caused by low environmental humidity, lack of liquid intake, or by the slowed metabolism of a chilled puppy. Be sure the puppies are receiving the proper amount of milk substitute and that the relative humidity in the puppies area is 55 to 65 percent. If the puppies are small and weak, the relative humidity may need to be as high as 85 percent. However, never couple an environmental temperature above 90° F. with a relative humidity above 90 percent; this sweltering combination could cause respiratory illness in the puppies.

Some signs of dehydration include listlessness, decreased appetite, and sticky mucous membranes in the puppy's mouth. If you suspect that a puppy is dehydrated, contact your vet immediately.

When and how should solid foods be introduced?

Starting as early as three weeks, you may feed the puppies semi-solid food. Blend dry or canned dog food with warm liquid-cow's milk, goat's milk, milk substitute, or water – until the food is the consistency of a thick milkshake. Put the gruel in a shallow bowl and place it near the puppies. Keep the puppies away from the dam for at least an hour before offering them the blended food; they will be hungrier and more likely to eat. Gradually reduce the amount of liquid, until the puppies are eating regular dog food by the age of eight weeks.

When and how does weaning proceed?

With the introduction of solid foods at about three weeks of age, the puppies will naturally and gradually begin to wean. To facilitate this process, you may want to keep the dam away from the puppies for gradually increasing periods of time. By eight weeks, they should be able to obtain all their nutrition and calories from canned or dry puppy food.

During weaning, continue to feed the dam twice her pre-pregnancy diet, gradually reducing the amount to normal by the time the puppies are eight weeks old.

How much weight should a puppy gain each day?

Generally, a puppy should be gaining weight daily at the rate of 1 ounce per 30 pounds of body weight expected at maturity. For example, if the puppy is expected to weigh 45 pounds at maturity, then he should be gaining about 1.5 ounces per day.

Also, as a general rule, the puppy's birth weight should double in eight to ten days. It is not wise, however, to overfeed in order to achieve these goals. Overfeeding can cause diarrhea and can also make the puppy grow into an obese adult.

It's a good idea to keep a record of each puppy's growth. Growth records serve two purposes: They allow you to track each puppy individually, which helps monitor proper growth and development. Also, if you become extremely involved in dog breeding, you will be able to understand the growth and development patterns of your bloodline through an examination of your records. (See Appendix for additional examples of records forms.)

When will the puppies' eyes open?

Puppies are born with their eyes closed. In about 10 to 14 days, their eyes will start to open. It's best to avoid exposing the newborns to direct light when their eyes begin opening, and for about 10 additional days as well.

Fig. 20A. Record of Puppy Weights

RECORD OF PUPPY WEIGHTS

SIRE_____ DAM_____

DATE WHELPED_____

NAME	Birth	weeks										months							1 y
		1	2	3	4	5	6	7	8	10	3	4	5	6	7	8	10	
Puppy A																		
Puppy B																		
Puppy C																		
Puppy D																		
Puppy E																		

Fig. 20B. Record of Individual Measurements

RECORD OF INDIVIDUAL MEASUREMENTS

NAME_____DATE WHELPED_____

SIRE _____DAM_____

TRAIT	weeks		months								1 yr.
	8	10	3	4	5	6	7	8	9	10	
HEIGHT											
Floor to Withers											
Floor to Elbow											
Elbow to Withers											
LENGTH											
Withers to Tailset											

When may the puppies' dewclaws be removed?

At about two to four days of age, you can take the puppies to your vet to have their dewclaws removed. Dewclaws are the rudimentary fifth toes on the insides of both the front and hind legs. If left in place, they may curl around and cut into the dog's skin, or they may catch on something and tear off.

Note, however, that the breed standards of some breeds, such as Great Pyrenees and Briards, require that the dewclaws be left untrimmed. With other breeds, dewclaw removal is either optional, or, required. Be sure to check your breed's current standard before having the dewclaws removed.

When and how is the tail docked?

Tail docking, also, is best done when the puppy is two to four days of age. Again, some breeds require tail docking and others do not. Be sure to check with your current breed standard before docking the puppies tails.

You may take the puppies to your vet to have their tails docked, or you may do it yourself. In either case, you must know the exact place to cut the tail. Most vets do not know the standards of each breed, so it is your responsibility to provide this information.

If you decide to dock the tails yourself, be sure to consult an experienced breeder. Better yet, try to arrange a time when you can watch the entire procedure before doing it yourself.

In preparation for tail docking, sterilize a pair of sharp scissors by boiling them in water for several minutes. Then place the scissors, along with one six-inch piece of clean string for each tail to be docked, into a dish of isopropyl alcohol. Have Monsel's solution or Kwik-Stop available to stop excess bleeding (stypic pencils); these can be purchased at your local drug store.

Next, tie the sterilized string onto the puppy's tail, just a little closer to the dog's hindquarters than where you are going to cut off the tail; this will form a tourniquet and help prevent blood loss. Next, cut the tail. This is painful to the puppy for a few seconds, so be sure to comfort the puppy as best you can. Then, apply stypic pencil to the end of the tail to help reduce bleeding and prevent infection. After two or three hours, remove the string and apply more stypic pencil.

Ear-cropping is a surgical procedure in which part of the ear leather is removed to induce the ear to stand erect. Some breed standards, such as those for Doberman Pinschers and Brussels Griffons, optionally allow dogs to have cropped ears.

Ear-cropping, if elected, may be performed when the puppy is eight to ten weeks old. After the ears are cropped, they need to be taped to a supportive mechanism for several weeks. This can be burdensome for you and uncomfortable for the puppy. Be sure to consider both the work and discomfort involved when deciding whether to crop your puppy's ears.

Many European countries have outlawed ear-cropping and tail-docking. They feel that the pain caused to the dog is unnecessary and cruel. If you feel the same, there are two other avenues to consider: you can either work within your breed to try to change the standard, or you may decide to switch to a breed which does not require or encourage tail-docking or ear-cropping.

When may the ears be cropped?

There are many diseases against which dogs can and should be immunized, including distemper, hepatitis, kennel cough, leptospirosis, and rabies. Your vet can provide you with a complete schedule of recommended vaccinations.

Generally, puppies need to receive their first vaccinations at six weeks of age. After receiving the full series of initial vaccinations, dogs need to be revaccinated annually against most of the above diseases.

When should the puppies receive their first vaccinations?

CHAPTER SUMMARY:

Puppies should nurse for four to six weeks.

Bottle-feeding and tube-feeding are the preferred methods of supplementing the dam's milk.

Beware of overfeeding a hand-fed puppy – overfeeding causes diarrhea and too rapid growth.

Orphaned puppies require assistance with feeding, elimination, maintaining body warmth, and guarding against dehydration.

Chilling is the leading cause of death in newborn puppies.

Introduce semi-solid gruel at about three weeks of age. Puppies should be completely weaned by eight weeks of age.

Each day a puppy should gain about one ounce per pound of expected adult weight.

A puppy's birth weight should double by 10 days of age.

Keep a record of each puppy's growth.

Puppies eyes start to open at about 10 to 14 days of age. Keep the newborns out of direct light while their eyes are opening, and for 10 days afterwards.

Puppies may have their dewclaws removed and their tails docked at two to four days of age. Ear-cropping may be performed at eight weeks of age.

Puppies should receive their first vaccinations at six weeks of age.

Understanding the Problems of Early Puppyhood

"coping with the headaches"

During the first eight or nine years that my late wife, Marjorie, and I were breeding dogs, we had no difficulties with stillbirths and deaths of newborn puppies. During this time, whenever we heard of another breeder who had lost puppies shortly after whelping, we were convinced that the losses were due to carelessness on the part of the breeder. After all, we were very careful, and we had no difficulties.

Suddenly, though, we started losing puppies. Our first losses occurred when one of our bitches whelped a litter of five. This particular dam had previously whelped two litters of six each, and had raised both litters with ease. We lost two puppies from this litter of five – a bitch and a male. In this particular breeding, we had wanted a bitch pup very much, and the bitch we lost was the one and only female in the litter. All of our breeding plans had to be put on hold.

We felt bad about those first losses, and we knew they were not due to carelessness. We also began to view our fellow breeder's losses with more compassion. Our next litter saw two survivors out of five puppies whelped.

Next we raised four out of six, which seemed to be an improvement. However, the next litter saw only one survivor out of five, and then we lost an entire litter of three. Losing that litter of three affected us deeply; we wanted to stop breeding rather than continue to subject ourselves to this type of discouragement.

As it turned out, our losses were all due to "Fading Puppy Syndrome." Of course, not all puppy losses are due to this particular cause. However, the more we talked with other breeders, the more we realized that we were not alone with this problem. Not all breeders would experience exactly the same symptoms, but the general pattern was quite similar: after years of successful, selective line-breeding, breeders would suddenly begin to lose puppies.

We decided that maybe an outcross would strengthen our bloodline, so we brought in an outside bitch and bred her to our primary stud dog. They produced a litter of four puppies, all of whom survived. Three of the four went on to earn their championships; two of them were Best-in-Show quality; and one of them was the greatest show dog we ever produced – he ranked in the top 10 of all breeds.

Even though we had felt like giving up, we persevered and ended up back on top of the dog show game. If you are losing puppies, read about the problem, talk to your veterinarian, seek advice from your fellow breeders, and try to find a solution. Your next litter may be your best! AG

What factors contribute most to the puppy's health and development?

Whether a puppy develops normally, before and after birth, depends entirely on environment and the hereditary characteristics handed down by the parents. A puppy's diet constitutes a major part of his environment; puppies that are fed inadequate, unbalanced diets fail to grow properly and may develop structural abnormalities and nutritional diseases, such as anemia and rickets. Other components of a puppy's environment include the diet and health of the dam during pregnancy and nursing, the presence of parasites, and the quality of care provided by both the dam and the breeder.

How does the prenatal environment affect the puppy's health?

An unfavorable prenatal environment may impede normal development before and after birth. The prenatal environment will probably be inadequate if the mother has been improperly cared for – a poor diet, lack of exercise, or a prevailing parasitic infestation.

Even though the gestation process provides the fetuses with first choice of the dam's nutrients, there must be something from which to choose; if the bitch

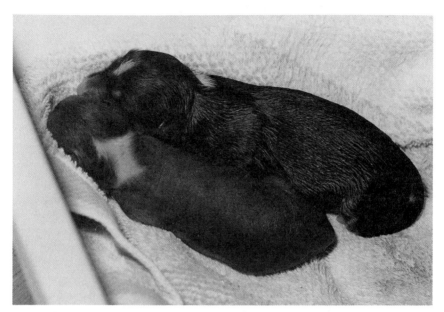

The newborns

is inadequately or improperly fed, the developing puppies will suffer. They may be so lacking in vitality as the result of malnutrition, that they will either be born dead, or will die shortly after birth.

Newborn puppies suffering from malnutrition do not necessarily look thin. They may be well formed and appear healthy. However, they may be so anemic and weak that they are unable to handle either the difficulties of being born or the external environment. Additionally, puppies that are born with worms acquired from the dam may not show signs of illness until they are three or four weeks of age. Because information concerning proper prenatal care of the bitch is readily available, malnutrition and parasites need not be major causes of puppy death.

It is estimated that about 28 percent of all puppies die in the first week after birth. Some of these puppies suffer from lethal congenital defects, maternal neglect, or accidents, such as being crushed in the whelping box. Following is a list of the most common causes of puppy death.

What are the most common causes of puppy death?

Internal Parasites. Puppies that are born with worms acquired from their dam may not show signs of illness until they are three or four weeks of age, then they may suddenly sicken and die. Some of the signs of worm infestation include: listlessness, diarrhea, weight loss, vomiting, dull, dry coat, and coughing. If your puppy exhibits any of these signs, see your vet immediately. Do not attempt to deworm a puppy yourself – it is too easy to miscalculate the amount of medication needed and to poison the puppy accidentally.

There are a wide variety of worms that can infest a puppy, including heartworms, roundworms, tapeworms, hookworms, and whipworms. All of these infestations are cured in the same way: the puppy is given a medicine which kills or expels the worms, but does not harm the puppy.

Injury. Injuries received either before or after birth may result in the death of one or more puppies in a litter, in spite of the fact that every precaution was taken to prevent such injuries. Sometimes the embryos may be crowded together too closely inside the uterus, prohibiting proper development. This may result in malformations, or in premature births of small, weak puppies. This is much more common in large litters, but may also occur in small- or average-size litters.

Carelessness on the part of a nervous or inexperienced bitch may account for the loss of some puppies that appear to be strong and healthy at birth. Even the most experienced bitch may occasionally sit or lie on a puppy, crushing or smothering him to death. A properly constructed whelping box will help reduce the mortality of newborn puppies.

Also, some dams may fail to retrieve a puppy that wanders away from the nest. The wandering puppy may then become chilled and weakened, so that even when he does manage to find his way back to the dam, he may be unable to compete with the stronger puppies for nursing. Therefore, a prospective brood bitch should be selected not only on the basis of her pedigree, conformation, and personality, but also on the basis of her ability – or on her ancestor's ability, if she herself has never had a litter – to whelp and raise a litter effectively.

Fading Puppies. A large percentage of neonatal puppy deaths can be attributed to a condition known as "Fading Puppy Syndrome." The fading puppy is one who is born malnourished because his dam received inadequate nutrition during gestation; is too weak to nurse effectively; is not receiving an adequate supply of milk; is in an environment that is not sufficiently warm; or, a combination of the above. Unless supplementary feeding is started within a few hours of birth, with frequent weight checks to monitor progress, and unless adequate heat is provided, these puppies will become chilled and weak, and will ultimately fade and die.

Sometimes, though, even the best of care will not save the fading puppy; he may simply have been born too weak to survive.

Neonatal Septicemia. Neonatal septicemia affects puppies from one to four days of age. This fatal condition is usually caused by a staphylococcus infection located in the vaginal tract of the bitch, and is transmitted to the puppy at birth. Sometimes, however, an unsanitary external environment is the precipitating factor in this disease.

Infected puppies will exhibit swollen abdomens with bluish discoloration on their flanks. They cry, are hypothermic and dehydrated, and refuse to nurse. Death occurs 12 to 18 hours after bloating and dehydration unless antibiotic treatment is started immediately. Also, supportive therapy (heat, glucose, and water) as described under Puppy Septicemia should be administered immediately as well.

Prevention involves a thorough pre-breeding veterinary examination with antibiotic therapy, if necessary, to counteract infection in the bitch. Kenneling should be scrupulously clean, as should everything else to which the newborn puppies are exposed, including your hands.

Puppy Septicemia. Puppy septicemia is the leading cause of death by disease in infant puppies, and occurs from four to forty days of age. It happens typically in vigorous puppies that were born normally and are efficient nursers.

The illness is sudden. First one puppy starts to cry – he has abdominal distension, diarrhea, and may have rapid respiration. Then the puppy refuses to nurse, becomes dehydrated, and loses weight rapidly. Death usually follows about 18 hours after the onset of symptoms. Then, another puppy becomes sick, then another and another. Septicemia can demolish most or all of a litter within five to six days.

This fatal illness in newborn puppies is caused by a bacterial infection, and is frequently associated with a metritis or mastitis infection in the bitch.

Metritis is a uterine infection that may be acute or chronic. In the acute phase, the dam becomes ill soon after the litter is whelped. She develops an abnormal vaginal discharge and a fever of up to 104° F. However, chronic metritis may not cause overt symptoms in the bitch and, in fact, may not be evidenced until she whelps stillborn puppies or puppies that succumb to infection shortly after birth.

Mastitis is a painful breast infection, and also produces a fever in the bitch. Both metritis and mastitis can transmit bacterial infections to the entire litter.

The sick puppies are chilled, have low blood sugar, and are dehydrated. Immediate steps must be taken to counteract these conditions or the puppies will die quickly. The puppies must be taken from the bitch, and the following actions must be taken immediately under the supervision of your vet:

1. For chilling: Because the puppy's body temperature has usually fallen to between 78° and 94° F, the puppy must be placed in an environmental temperature of 85° to 90° F. until its body temperature has slowly and carefully risen to normal. You may warm the puppy with an incubator, heat lamp, or heating pad.

   Stimulate the puppy's circulation by frequently turning and massaging him during this slow warming process – only the surfaces of the puppy's body will be warmed if this careful massaging and turning is not done. The newborn puppy's temperature can be taken with an infant's rectal thermometer. Hold up the base of the puppy's tail and insert the thermometer one-half inch into the rectum. The environmental temperature can be monitored with an inside thermometer on the floor of the whelping box or incubator.

The relative humidity should be 55 to 60 percent; this can be accomplished by using a home humidifier in the room in which the whelping box is kept.

2. For low blood sugar: The sick puppy's blood sugar must be increased rapidly. Administering a glucose solution that is absorbed directly into the stomach is the best way of doing this. Give the puppy 5 to 15 percent glucose in water, orally, 1 to 2 cc. (milliliters) every half hour. As the puppy's condition improves, gradually increase the dosage to 5 to 6 cc.

3. For dehydration: The glucose and water therapy described above should also be sufficient to rehydrate the ailing puppy. If the puppy's condition is dire, the vet may want to administer subcutaneous hydrating solutions.

In some cases, the vet may also wish to treat the puppies with antibiotics. However, it is urgent that you consult with your vet before beginning the puppies on a course of treatment for septicemia.

Canine Herpes Virus. Herpes is another leading cause of death in young puppies. Herpes is transmitted at whelping as puppies pass through the vagina of an infected dam. Puppies can also be infected by littermates or infected adult dogs. The disease is usually fatal if contracted by puppies during the first three weeks of life. Older puppies with herpes virus usually develop mild upper respiratory infections from which recovery is uneventful.

Affected puppies have soft, green, odorless bowel movements; this is usually the first symptom. They may vomit or retch, have shallow respiration that becomes gasping as the disease progresses, and they may refuse to nurse. The puppies will cry pitifully and continuously.

Susceptibility of infant puppies is thought to be caused by their low body temperature. The canine herpes virus has been shown to multiply optimally at temperatures of 94° to 97° F., that of the neonatal puppy. The virus grows poorly at the body temperature of the adult dog.

Keeping puppies in a high environmental temperature for 24 hours is the only effective treatment; but even this is problematical. For three hours the environmental temperature must be 100°. The puppies also need glucose solution administered orally every 15 minutes to prevent dehydration. (Refer to the section on Puppy Septicemia for information about administering glucose therapy.) Then the temperature can be reduced to 90° for the remainder of the 24-hour period. If the puppies survive the treatment, chances are they will also survive the disease.

Treatment is not advised, however, if a puppy has already started to cry. This indicates that hemorrhaging has started and survival is doubtful. If this puppy should live, chronic kidney disease may develop during his first year of life.

Kennels in which herpes virus is a recurring problem should take preventive action by having their vets inject neonatal puppies with gamma globulin serum.

Toxic Milk Syndrome. Bacterial toxins in the dam's milk, caused by incomplete emptying of the uterus during whelping, produce toxic effects in puppies less than two weeks old. The sick puppies cry, are bloated, have diarrhea, and also have red, swollen, and protruding rectums.

The infected puppies should be taken from the bitch, placed in a warm environment, and fed a solution of 5 to 15 percent glucose in water, until the bloating has subsided. After that, feed these puppies a milk substitute until they are returned to the dam.

The bitch should be treated with appropriate medication to cleanse the uterus, and also with antibiotics to prevent infection. The puppies can be returned to her as soon as her treatment has been initiated by your vet.

Canine Parvovirus. Canine parvovirus exists in two forms: "enteric," or diarrhea form, and "myocardial," or cardiac form. This section is concerned just with the myocardial form, since puppies are normally its exclusive victims.

A puppy infected with myocardial parvovirus will

abruptly sicken and die; in fact, the puppy will often be discovered already dead. For this reason, once a puppy displays any symptoms of myocardial parvovirus – including refusal to nurse, crying, and retching – it is of utmost importance that the puppy be treated by a vet immediately.

The asymptomatic littermates should also be seen by the vet because there's a good chance they are infected as well.

The primary source of infection is contaminated dog feces, and the virus is easily disseminated on the feet of both humans and dogs. The virus is resistant to not only heat, detergent, and alcohol, but has been known to live in dog feces for more than three months.

However, the virus can be killed by a mixture of one part chlorine bleach to 30 parts water. It's a good idea to wash down the kenneling area with this chlorine mixture once parvovirus has been contracted. However, sanitation alone cannot completely halt the spread of this virus; therefore, be certain that your puppies receive parvovirus vaccinations as part of their immunization program.

If the bitch has antibodies to parvovirus – as a result of either a previous infection or a vaccination – she may transfer these helpful antibodies to her puppies through the placenta and the colostrum. (See the glossary for definitions of placenta and colostrum.) This maternal antibody protects the newborns during the first five weeks when they are the most susceptible to the myocardial form of parvovirus.

How can I reduce the occurrence of puppy death?

Most puppy deaths are preventable. The main factors in preventing puppy death include: selection of sound breeding stock; a healthy, well-nourished bitch; clean kenneling; adequate heat for the dam and her litter; careful supervision of puppies' early weight gains; and, prompt veterinary assistance if puppies start to fade, cry, or have any of the early symptoms of puppy diseases.

CHAPTER SUMMARY:

The major factors contributing to a puppy's health and development are the prenatal environment, the puppy's diet, the elimination of parasites, the cleanliness of the kennel, and the quality of care provided by both the dam and the breeder.

A poor prenatal environment may prevent a puppy from developing normally, both before and after birth.

Statistics show that more than one puppy out of four usually dies in the first week after birth.

Some of the common causes of puppy death include injury, internal parasites, and disease.

When a puppy displays any signs of illness, such as coughing, vomiting, listlessness, diarrhea, swelling, or crying, immediately consult your vet. Sometimes, a puppy can be saved if he receives treatment quickly.

Keep puppy death to a minimum through the selection of sound breeding stock, good prenatal care, a clean, warm kennel for the dam and her puppies, careful supervision of puppies' weight gains, and, if necessary, immediate veterinary assistance.

Evaluating and Selling the Puppies

"sharp eye and a quick mind required"

If you're going to be a successful breeder, you must be able to assess properly your puppies and quickly sell those who don't qualify as top show-quality stock. If you cannot do this, you become bogged down with a group of "could've been" puppies. Your costs for maintaining them rises and their saleability goes down as they lose their cuteness and appeal to the pet-buying public.

You must also learn the basics of salesmanship and merchandising so you can move those cute and cuddly puppies early. You must then combine your evaluation talents with your salesmanship skills to sell those show prospects to the right show people.

If you can do this, you will have completed the ring of all things necessary to become a winner – go for it!
AG

Most breeders, after years of breeding within one bloodline, are reasonably able to predict the development and outcome of each puppy in a litter. Typically, they can estimate a puppy's ultimate size, when a puppy will go through its awkward phase, and whether or not the puppy can be considered show quality.

Most of the time, breeders base their predictions both on gut feeling as well as their many years of experience. However, there is a way to assess each puppy's potential without having had many years of dog-breeding experience. By maintaining careful

Can breeders predict the outcome of each puppy in a litter?

Dreaming of the future

records of their puppies' developmental stages, breeders can quickly begin to understand the maturation process of their own bloodline. For example, they may discover that most of their puppies go through an awkward stage between three and eight months of age, or they may find that their puppies generally reach adult height at 10 months.

However, no system is foolproof. Puppies that start off looking like excellent show prospects may end up being only pet quality. Or a puppy may be sold as pet quality, and then end up a top winner in the show ring. It is impossible to predict the outcome of each puppy with 100 percent accuracy. But, by maintaining accurate, detailed records, a breeder can substantially improve the odds.

To assist in predicting the puppies' potentials, breeders should record accurately the weights and measurements of each puppy in every litter, including weight, height (floor to withers, and floor to elbow), and length (withers to tailset, point of shoulder to tailset). These measurements should be taken at birth, two weeks, four weeks, and then every four weeks until maturity is reached.

What sort of developmental records should breeders maintain?

Fig. 21. Points of Measurements (A to F; B to B prime; A to B; A to A square; A prime to A square)

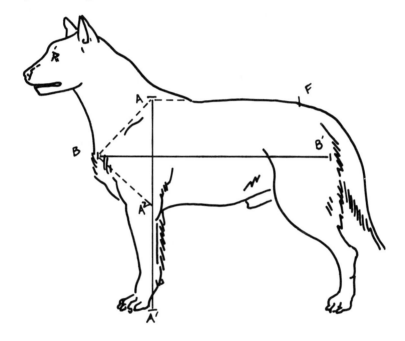

Also, notes on head development, heaviness of bone, and personality should be recorded, as well as any other features the breeder may wish to track.

After raising several litters, breeders should be able to perceive and identify the patterns of growth and development in their bloodlines, and they should be able to answer the following types of questions with a measurable degree of accuracy:

1. At what age will this puppy attain ultimate size?

Measuring growth

2. At what age will this puppy attain ultimate development?
3. Can ultimate size be predicted by size at birth?
4. Do puppies in this bloodline go through growth spurts?
5. When will the growth spurts most likely occur?
6. Will one part of the body develop sooner than another part?
7. Will this puppy go through an awkward stage? If so, when?

The ability to answer questions such as these can help breeders predict the development of each puppy and determine which puppies can be considered the best show prospects.

Development is always easier to predict if the breeder is dealing within one bloodline. When new

Measuring growth

bloodlines are added to the genetic maze, both development and outcome will probably be different from previous results.

Most puppies go through an awkward stage. Their bodies stop being cuddly as they take on an adolescent appearance, becoming gangly "teenagers." Fortunately, most puppies emerge unscathed from this stage, and eventually redisplay most of their original promise. However, there are some who never live up to the desired potential.

Some puppies do not go through this phase: they maintain beauty, balance, and proportion throughout their first year. These puppies, often called "flyers," outshine their gangly siblings. If one of these rare individuals comes along, let's hope you will recognize and treasure him. Don't overlook his awkward littermates, however, for sometimes they can also develop into outstanding show dogs.

Do all puppies go through an awkward stage?

It is impossible to predict the exact timing of a puppy's awkward stage. It can start as early as eight weeks, but may not start until the puppy is three or four months old. Most puppies are out of the awkward stage by the time they are eight months old, but some puppies emerge from this stage as early as six or seven months.

When does the awkward stage occur?

Generally, the timing of the awkward stage is consistent within the same bloodline. For example, from past experience with a particular bloodline, a breeder could determine that the progeny of that bloodline usually experience the awkward stage between three and seven months of age. Knowing when to expect the awkward stage and how long it typically lasts can help reduce the amount of anxiety felt by the breeder. This breeder may mentally lock the puppy away until he is seven months old, and then pull him out for reevaluation.

The two main causes of the awkward stage in puppies are their rapid rate of growth and dentition (the loss of baby teeth and subsequent replacement with adult teeth). During this time, the puppy's head and body may lose their previous beauty and balance.

What happens during the awkward stage?

Fortunately, the head and body usually begin to improve as the puppy approaches maturity. Generally, the improvement becomes noticeable at about six months of age, and continues until the original lines and proportion have been restored.

If the head stays in balance during the awkward stage, the puppy's head will probably turn out nicely. If, however, the head loses its original balance, the puppy may not grow into a top-quality show dog. Some breeders have been able to abolish the awkward, or "plaining out," phase in their stock through selective breeding. Their puppies never go through this phase; their heads are good as tiny puppies, and they remain that way.

The rapid rate of growth during this time can cause many puppies to develop awkward, uncoordinated bodies. To make matters worse, different parts of the body can develop at different times. One puppy's legs may develop before his chest, giving him an "up-on-leg" look; he may walk around on stilts for months before finally filling in. Another pup may develop his forechest early; this may cause him to look low-to-the-ground and "dumpy" until his legs catch up.

Usually the body parts even out by the time maturity is reached, but not always. Many a breeder's dreams have been shattered by a puppy whose development just never caught up with his early promise. When this happens, try to take it in stride; learn from experience which dogs to pin your hopes on.

When should a breeder evaluate the puppies?

A good rule of thumb for beginning breeders is to evaluate puppies at eight weeks of age, before the onset of the awkward phase. At this time puppies usually will reflect their adult potential more accurately than later, during the awkward phase. More experienced breeders can draw from past experiences to determine the appropriate timing for assessing puppies from their bloodlines.

What should the breeder look for when evaluating the puppies?

When appraising eight-week-old puppies, rank most highly those with overall balance rather than those with a few great parts. For example, imagine you are comparing two puppies. The first has a great

Fig. 22. Critique of a Litter

Such Charm

Such Class

Such Brass

Such A Corker

5½ weeks: At this age, all four puppies looked like peas in a pod...great heads and good coats...neck and shoulders were good and all appeared short-backed...Such A Corker's head piece was outstanding...we felt we had a litter of all champions...which one was best? Only time would tell.

Such Charm

Such Class

Such Brass

Such A Corker

7 weeks: From a litter of four all appeared to be outstanding young prospects...at this stage, Hi-Boots Such A Corker was the leading candidate to be the pick of the litter...he was beautifully marked as a Black/Tan, had good bone and substance and his conformation, except for a slight steepness of shoulder, was excellent...he had a plush head with very good ear set...his coat was full and thick...he measured one inch shorter down the back than his height at the withers.

Hi-Boots Such Class was a thick, heavyset black puppy with a massive head that had potential, but seemed to lack chiseling...an excellent coat, neck...shoulders were good but a bit heavy...a short back and very strong, well-developed thighs...overall, he had good balance, one part blending well with the others...just seemed "too much"...he measured 1½ inches shorter down the back than his height at the withers.

Hi-Boots Such Brass was a substantial dog, less thick throughout than his black brother, but excellent bone and substance...poorly marked but had markings in all the right places...thick and luxurious coat...head was plush with excellent chiseling...measured the same down the back as his height.

Hi-Boots Such Charm was a black bitch with a beautiful head whose bone and substance was in proportion to her size...she appeared to be small but plush-looking with less coat than her brothers...the best neck and shoulders of the litter...she measured ¾ inches shorter down the back than her height at the withers.

At this stage, Such A Corker was rated as the best puppy with Such Class a close second. Such Brass was very promising, but seemed not to be all together yet.

Such Charm

Such Class

Such Brass

Such A Corker

12 weeks: The tide had taken a definite turn...Such Brass's markings were much clearer and he had knit together...when on the ground, he handled himself like a master hunter...light on his feet and seemed very assured...his coat was thick and luxurious and his head was something breeders dreamed about.

Such Class had also come into his own...he was now better chiseled and had grown into his thick, square frame...an excellent topline and still the great bone and substance...on the ground, he too seemed to move with grace.

Such A Corker stayed where he had been at 7 weeks...still good but the other two males had passed him...on the ground he seemed awkward in comparison with the others...his gait was more plodding while they seemed to float.

Such Charm was not going to make it as a show dog...her head was still beautiful, but she was beginning to show signs of a greater length of body and no apparent improvement in coat.

Such Brass   Such A Corker

At 6 months, we had two flyers: Such Class and Such Brass. Such A Corker was still a finishable dog, but compared to the other two he was a plodder. Such Charm had been sold as a pet. Her coat had not come in and her length of back was excessive. This was a fault in the line we wished to eliminate.

At 7 months, Such Brass was so mature looking that he was entered in the open class at the largest Cocker Specialty on the West Coast and went up for a five-point major. He finished at 10 months with four majors. Such Brass went on to win 100 Best of Varieties out of 125 times shown. Out of 90 all-breed shows in which he was entered, he placed in the group 76 times. He sired 37 champions and was twice tied for the top-producing dog of the year in his breed.

At 10 months, in his first show, Such Class went Best of Breed at a large Specialty show and placed in the group three times en route to finishing with four majors, losing only once when he went reserve winners. He was never specialed.

Such A Corker finished his championship at 2½. He had a modest show career.

The changes we saw as the puppies matured was a marked increase in chiseling and head development in Such Class and Such Brass. They never went through the classical awkward stages like Such A Corker and Such Charm. Corker and Charm both lost their chiseling and lengthened in back as they went from 12 weeks to 6 months. They looked like gawky teenagers while the other two looked suave and sleek.

Our experience tables, upon reflection, indicated that Such Class would turn out the way he did. Other puppies from similar breedings had followed that pattern and were early champions. How good he would be did not become evident until he was about 7 months of age. Such Charm followed the mold exactly. We knew she wasn't going to make it early on. Such Brass was a sleeper. His measurements led us to believe he would conform to our norms and be a good dog. However, at 12 weeks he magically began to emerge, especially when one watched him on the ground playing with the other puppies. He was fearless as was Such Class. Such A Corker was definitely a follower.

head and spectacular markings, but is a little weak in the body and coat, and seems a bit shy. The second has a pleasing appearance: nice – but not great – head, good coat and body, and a winning personality. Which has the greater likelihood of success in the show ring? Though the first has a better head, the second possesses overall symmetry and balance, plus an outgoing demeanor. Therefore, the second has greater show potential.

Base a puppy's evaluation not only on how he looks in a show pose, but also on how he looks while moving on the ground. There are several reasons for doing this. First of all, when arranging the puppy in a show pose, you may inadvertently manipulate the puppy into looking better than he is; you may actually end up deceiving yourself. Also, you need to see how the puppy moves and how he handles himself with other puppies. The best "movers" are the ones who are well-coordinated, who can cut and turn easily, and who appear light and nimble.

Along with a puppy's physical appearance, you also need to consider his personality. A dog must have a certain magical spark to be a top winner. This elusive spark of personality adds life and spunk to an otherwise empty, though lovely, animal. Without it, a dog may never be able to handle himself with confidence in the ring. A winning dog is flashy in appearance and spirit. He prances into the ring and says, "Look at me, aren't I something!"

How can the breeder help puppies achieve their potential?

In order for any show-quality puppy to fulfill his early promise, his environment must provide all the necessary conditions to ensure ultimate growth and development, both physical and mental. The person responsible for providing such an environment is, of course, the breeder or the owner.

A puppy's first contact with the world can have a significant effect upon his later development. Some bitches are simply poor mothers and are unable to get their puppies off to a good start. Luckily, normal, healthy puppies that do get off to a poor start will usually catch up with those that are in a more positive environment. They may not grow as quickly, and their growing period will usually be longer, but by the time they reach maturity, there should be little difference in size.

The same usually holds true for the older puppy that has received a setback due to illness. Growth may be halted temporarily during the illness, but such puppies have been known to make up that period of growth at a later date. Many breeders are tempted to write off puppies such as these – and many do, only to discover later that they made a mistake.

The quantity and quality of food a puppy receives is vitally important; poor nutrition can result in a puppy's failure to live up to its potential. The limits of a puppy's eventual size, bone, and development have been predetermined by heredity. This development can either be fully realized through proper nutrition, or never reached because of poor nutrition.

Because appetite and eating are important habits, the good eaters are one step ahead in developing their potential. On the other hand, the poor eater may be penalized through his own lack of effort. One of the most difficult tasks imaginable is to get the poor eater to develop properly. Any possible physical cause of lack of healthy appetite, such as infected tonsils, or worms, should be investigated thoroughly. Unfortunately, there are some puppies that will never eat more than what is required for marginal subsistence.

A puppy who is a good eater will often be a bit chubby. Should this puppy go through the awkward stage, his awkwardness will be more pronounced than that of his slimmer littermates – the chubby puppy usually loads up in the shoulder, and looks soft, sloppy, and cumbersome. The unknowing owner gives up on this specimen and dismisses him before a diet has had a chance to work. It is important to note that extreme obesity can cause permanent structural damage in a puppy.

At the other extreme, the too-thin puppy, while retaining a semblance of his original promise, often will never fill out enough to make a good show dog. This puppy will often appear frail – for lack of nutrition can have an adverse effect on physical well-being. This puppy, too, may be discarded as a

Measuring up

potential show dog without the owner attempting to uncover the causes of his diminished appetite.

Breeds in which an outgoing personality and good disposition are highly desirable, breeders must help develop their dogs' personalities. A show specimen must have something more than physical beauty – the show dog must possess "heart." Without this extra spark of personality, the most perfect specimen is nothing more than a shell. The responsibility for developing personality and disposition is just as important as providing food and medical care. The personality problems of most shy, snapping, wetting puppies can usually be traced to environmental factors rather than to inherited ones.

How do I sell the puppies I decide not to keep?

As soon as you know that your bitch is in whelp, spread the word that you may soon have some puppies for sale. Talk to your acquaintances at dog club meetings, and also to owners and exhibitors at dog shows. Often, they will know of people who want to buy a puppy of your breed.

After the puppies are eight weeks old, advertise them in the newspaper, placing an ad that states the breed, sex, quality, age, price, and your phone number. For example:

> For Sale: AKC Standard Poodles, White, 8 wks old, 2 males $150, 1 show-potential female $400, 321-1111.

Base your asking price on the current going price in your region.

Once you are an established breeder, you may also wish to advertise your show-quality puppies in dog magazines and newspapers. In your ad, be sure to emphasize the winning and producing records of the puppies' ancestors. For example, you may want to state that the puppies' sire has won three best-in-shows, and produced a total of 16 champion offspring.

Also, if the sire or dam is owned by you but was bred by another breeder, be sure to preface the dog's AKC-registered name with your kennel name. For example, suppose the dog was bred by "Jolly" kennels, and his AKC-registered name is Ch. Jolly's Jellyroll.

Suppose further that your kennel's name is "Westwind." Since you are now the owner of the dog, in the ad you should refer to the dog as Westwind's Ch. Jolly's Jellyroll. This way, people will associate your kennel name with the dog.

Be prepared to handle phone inquiries, written inquiries, and visitors to the kennel. For phone inquiries, keep nearby a handy checklist of information about each puppy, as well as a copy of the pedigree. Because the prospective buyer cannot see your facial expressions, you might want to use expressive words to describe the puppy and to convey your enthusiasm – words such as "stunning topline," or "outstanding coat." However, be careful not to misrepresent the dog; do not omit the faults your puppy may have, though there is no need to stress them.

You can answer written inquiries with a phone call if prospective buyers seem well informed, anxious to buy, and if it seems that you have the dog they're looking for. Otherwise, answer written inquiries promptly in writing. Remember, again, to convey enthusiasm by using expressive, descriptive words. You may also want to include a color photograph of the puppies that are for sale. Once your kennel is well-established, you may wish to make up a brochure about the kennel and insert a handwritten note about the dogs you currently have for sale.

When prospective buyers come to your kennel, make sure that all the dogs are clean and groomed, and that the kennel is tidy and attractive. Most kennel visitors have already decided that they want a dog, and once they actually see and touch the adorable, cuddly puppies, they will have a hard time resisting the purchase of one. Therefore, you do not need to use high-pressure sales tactics to sell your puppies; your main job is to not dissuade them from purchasing.

One common sales mistake is to deride the competition by speaking badly of other breeders in the area. This only serves to make the buyer concerned about your integrity, and it may even push the buyer into defending, and perhaps purchasing from the other breeder. Another sales mistake is to quarrel with prospective buyers. Avoid arguments, even if the buyers are misinformed about the breed or are unappreciative of the quality of your puppies. Listen attentively to their concerns, and express your own opinions courteously. You are interested in selling your puppies, not in engaging in long-winded debates about other breeds or other breeders.

It is the breeder's duty to evaluate carefully all prospective buyers. Make certain that the buyer will provide a loving and suitable home for the new puppy, and that the buyer's home and lifestyle will suit your particular breed. For instance, large hunting dogs need a sizable, fenced backyard or to be taken for long walks several times a day. It may be necessary for you to find out if the buyers have a fenced yard or small children, or whether the dog will have companionship during the day.

How do I screen prospective buyers?

Typical pet quality

If you are selling a pet-quality dog, you may wish for it to not be shown, because your kennel name would then be associated with poor quality. To ensure that the dog not be shown, you may sell the dog without its AKC registration papers, or with a spay/ neuter contract. Of course, this reduces the selling price of the dog, and explains why pet-quality dogs – even purebreds – are less expensive than their show-quality littermates.

On the other hand, if you are selling a show-quality dog, you may want to be certain that the new owners will indeed show it. By selling to someone who is already involved in the dog show game, someone who shares your commitment to showing dogs, you can be fairly certain that your puppy will be shown to his best advantage. Sometimes buyers will come along who have no previous experience with showing purebred dogs, but who seem genuinely committed to succeeding in the dog game. You may want to ask why they want a show dog, how many dog shows they have attended, and if they grew up with dogs. Ultimately, though, you may have to rely upon your own intuition when deciding whether to sell a top-quality show dog to a prospective buyer.

As a professional breeder, you need to provide a written sales contract that outlines the conditions of sale. This contract should spell out clearly and simply the agreement reached.

What should be in the sales contract?

Some terms commonly contained in dog sales contracts include:

- A requirement that the dog be well cared for. A conscientious breeder will usually provide a book on care and training to the novice owner. Also, to make sure the purchaser stays on the right track, the breeder may offer future consultations.
- A guarantee that the dog being sold is free from the genetic faults prevalent in the breed. The contract should state clearly that if any genetic faults surface, such as hip dysplasia, the owner will be compensated with cash or with a replacement puppy. The contract should also state that a second veterinary opinion may be requested in case of controversy.
- A statement that the dog is not guaranteed to be show-quality or breeding-stock.
- The basic requirements that the dog's new owner must fulfill before showing or breeding the dog. For example, that the dog be free from major genetic faults, be in good health, and be bred only to a dog of the breeder's choosing.

There should be some flexibility in the contract, allowing the breeder to refund the sales price instead of replacing the dog. This may occur if the buyers failed to represent themselves honestly or failed to treat the animal well. The last thing a conscientious breeder would want is to provide a buyer with another animal to mistreat.

On some specific bitch sales, the breeder might wish to sign the AKC registration papers as co-owner. This helps to ensure that the terms of the contract are kept, because the signatures of both owners are required to register that bitch's puppies. For example, suppose you produce a show-quality bitch puppy and then sell her. As part of the sales agreement, you may

Fig. 23. Example of a Sales Agreement and Guarantee

PUPPY SALES AGREEMENT AND GUARANTEE
(May be used for Pet Sales/Show Sales/Co-Ownerships)

THIS AGREEMENT is made and entered into this ____ day of
_____ 19____, by and between _____
of _____ , (City, State), hereinafter called SELLER/BREEDER,
and _____ of _____ ,
hereinafter called BUYER.

WITNESSETH:

WHEREAS, Seller agrees to sell and hereby does sell the following
described dog, delivered to Buyer on the ____ day of _____, 19____:
Breed _____ AKC No. _____ Sex ____ Born _____
Color _____
Sire _____
Dam _____
Name _____ Tattoo _____

WHEREAS, Seller guarantees the above dog to be in good health
and free of disease for 48 hours after date of delivery,

NOW THEREFORE, in consideration of the covenants and prom-
ises as hereinafter set forth, and other good and valuable consideration, the parties do hereby agree as follows:

1. BUYER has paid SELLER the sum of _____ , and receipt
thereof is hereby acknowledged; BUYER AGREES to pay to Seller the
additional sum of _____ by the ____ day of _____.

2. ADDITIONAL TERMS: _____
_____
_____
_____
_____
_____
_____

3. Said dog may be shown on the following terms: _____
_____

4. Breeding expenses to be paid as follows: _____
_____

5. Buyer agrees and binds himself to take good and reasonable
care of said dog; feed and house him properly, control him when off
his premises and to avoid loss by theft, running away, damage by
other dogs or otherwise, and to promptly secure the best of veterinary attention to the physical welfare of said dog for the duration of
the term of this agreement. Buyer is responsible for all medical
expenses that may be incurred on behalf of said dog. Buyer agrees to
hold Seller harmless from any damages to property, other dogs or

persons that may be caused by said dog. Buyer further agrees that if he does not desire to keep said dog for any reason at any time prior to completion of conditions herein, Seller shall have first priority to claim said dog as follows: _____

Buyer further states that he has a fenced yard and agrees that he will not chain, tie or otherwise mistreat the said dog. Buyer agrees if said dog is returned to Seller, Buyer will execute AKC registration to sole ownership of Seller; and that said dog will be up-to-date on all vaccinations and in as good health as when dog was sold to Buyer.

6. Buyer understands that this dog is sold as _____ and guaranteed as stated herein.

7. Buyer agrees and understands that if any conditions herein are not completed as set forth: Seller has the right to repossess said dog forthwith and Buyer shall not be entitled to any refund of any monies paid to Seller pursuant to the agreement contained herein. Under such circumstances, Buyer agrees to relinquish his interest in said dog and to execute the AKC registration certificate to the sole ownership of Seller. Buyer agrees that in the event litigation in a court of law becomes necessary, Seller may request damages in addition to the value of dog, attorney's fees and costs incurred.

Buyer's initials _____
Seller's initials _____

8. When all conditions set forth herein have been completed, Seller shall execute the AKC registration certificate to sole ownership of Buyer.

9. Seller states the said dog has received the following: (Health)
_____
_____
_____
_____

GUARANTEE:
10. Seller guarantees that the above dog will x-ray normal or better, at age of two (2) years, or dog will be replaced with another dog of similar quality and breeding when available, upon the following terms and conditions:

(a) That said dog has not been used for breeding without the consent and knowledge of Seller; and

(b) That a copy of the OFA certification or other radiologist report (qualified radiologist ONLY) shall be provided to Seller; and

(c) Provided said dog has received proper exercise, vitamins, proper diet as prescribed by Seller, and has been properly maintained for his size and weight; and

(d) No hip X-ray prior to two (2) years of age shall be considered pertinent to this guarantee; and

(e) that notice of neutering executed in writing by a vet, is sent to Seller within thirty (30) days of the date of (b) above; and

(f) that Seller is given the opportunity to reclaim said dog if desired and/or make arrangements mutually agreed upon by Buyer and Seller as circumstances warrant.

11. Seller guarantees that if said dog is being sold to Buyer as "show quality," then said dog is guaranteed to be a proper representative of the breed in accordance with the AKC breed standard, provided the said dog has been properly maintained for his size and weight, fed the diet and vitamins as prescribed by Seller, so that he may reach his full potential as set forth in the breed standard. If said dog does not fulfill the requirements in this paragraph by 18 months of age, said dog shall be replaced with another dog of similar quality and breeding when available. This guarantee shall be null and void if said dog has been used for breeding. Buyer and Seller shall further mutually agree whether said dog shall be returned to Seller, neutered, or other terms mutually agreed upon between the parties hereto.

Other known hereditary problems (eyes, testicles, bites, etc.) detected in said dog will be handled in the same manner as hip problems.

_____

_____

_____

12. The sum of _____ ($ _____)
DOLLARS will be refunded to Buyer upon written proof of neutering by a qualified veterinarian if said dog is neutered within _____ months hereof. This clause is null and void if said dog is used for breeding without consent of Seller.

BY AFFIXING HIS SIGNATURE BELOW, BUYER(S) UNDERSTAND AND APPROVE THE PROVISIONS AND TERMS STATED HEREINABOVE, CLAUSES #1-12, AND AGREES THERETO.

_____   _____
Buyer   Buyer

Address: _____

_____   Phone: _____

_____   Your Kennel Name
Seller/Breeder   Name
                                     Address & Phone

stipulate that you select the sire of her first litter, and that you be given first choice to purchase any puppy in that litter. The only way to guarantee these rights is to write them into the sales contract, and to have yourself listed as co-owner. Then, when the terms of the contract are met – that is, when you have selected your puppy from the bitch's first litter – you may relinquish co-ownership of the bitch.

Fig. 24. Example of an AKC Withholding Agreement

A.K.C. REGISTRATION WITHHOLDING AGREEMENT

Date: _____

The undersigned fully understands and agrees that the purchase of the within described dog is for the purposes of a family pet ONLY and the dog is not to be used for breeding or show, other than obedience. The undersigned further agrees that they are not to receive the American Kennel Club registration papers on the said dog and said papers are being withheld by the Seller of said dog until such time as a certificate from a veterinarian is presented to the Seller within _____ of the date of this agreement, as proof that the said dog has been neutered, at which time the A.K.C. registration papers will then be delivered to the undersigned Buyer AFTER SAID DATE, registration papers will be returned to the A.K.C. with a copy of this agreement.

The Seller hereby certifies that the within described dog is healthy and free from disease, and guarantees said health for a period of forty-eight (48) hours from the date of this agreement.

It is further understood and agreed if the Buyer(s) do not desire to keep the said dog, it shall be returned to the Seller in a good and healthy condition and the purchase price will be applied toward the purchase of another dog, of the same type and value, when available, unless other arrangements are made. UNDER NO CIRCUMSTANCES, shall the said dog be offered for sale or given away to anyone, until the Seller has been contacted.

As it is understood by the Buyer that said dog is being sold as "pet quality," no further guarantees other than immediate health status are offered.

The Seller of the said dog shall have the prerogative of re-evaluating the said dog, if requested by the Buyer. In the event said dog is considered breeding quality or conformation quality, this agreement shall become null and void and a new agreement shall be effected. IT IS AGREED THAT ONLY THE SELLER SHALL HAVE THE AUTHORITY TO RE-EVALUATE SAID DOG.

Breed _____ AKC No. _____ Sex ____ Born _____
Color _____

Sire _____
Dam _____
Name _____ Tattoo _____
Other Identifying Marks: _____

Other Comments: _____
_____
_____

WE HAVE READ AND UNDERSTAND AND AGREE TO THE ABOVE AGREEMENT, AND SIGNED SAME THIS ____ day of _____, 19____.

SELLER: BUYER:

Name   _____

Address   _____

Phone   Phone: _____

_____   _____
(Signature)   (Signature)

Two youngsters

Withholding of AKC registration papers is a good way to ensure that a pet-quality puppy is not bred.

Stephanie Vargo, assistant editor of AKC *Gazette*, stated in the May 1991 issue:

"Since 1989, another alternative is available. It is called the Limited Registration option. Under this AKC approved method a breeder may have the dog issued a Limited Registration certificate which states the dog is not currently eligible for registration. Though originally intended to be used solely in the sale of pet quality pups, breeders have found applications for limited registrations for 'borderline' pups and show prospects, too. Limited registration offers the breeders who feel that at eight weeks it is too difficult to determine the quality of a pup, limited registration gives them a grace period in which they can monitor the dog's progress and change to full registration when appropriate."

No matter how scrupulously you screen prospective buyers, there may be some irresponsible people who do not fulfill their end of the bargain. More often than not, it's the breeding arrangement that is broken. If the dog is sold to out-of-town buyers, it is difficult to ensure that the terms of the agreement are fulfilled. It is much easier to monitor a contract when the buyer resides in your area.

Although most states have laws that protect the buyer against deceit and fraud, protection for the seller is much harder to come by. Therefore, to protect yourself and your dog, make sure the contract states: "Breech of any terms of this contract entitles the seller to repossession." This way, you have legal ground to repossess your dog if you feel he is being mistreated or misused.

CHAPTER SUMMARY:

By maintaining accurate, detailed records of the growth and development of each puppy, a novice breeder can quickly learn to understand the developmental phases of his bloodline.

Most puppies go through an awkward stage. This

stage usually begins at two to three months of age, and lasts until the puppy is about six or seven months old.

The main causes of the awkward stage are dentition and rapid growth.

Beginning breeders should first evaluate their puppies at about eight weeks of age. When evaluating the puppies, rank most highly those with overall balance and symmetry, rather than those with one or two outstanding features.

Evaluate the puppies in a "stacked" show pose, as well as while moving on the ground.

A show dog needs an extra "spark" of extroverted personality to succeed in the ring.

The dog's genetic potential is set at conception; it is then the breeder's responsibility to make certain that dog reaches his potential.

Advertise your puppies for sale in local newspapers and by word-of-mouth at dog shows and dog club meetings.

Be prepared to handle phone inquiries, written inquiries, and visitors to your kennel.

Carefully evaluate all prospective buyers. Make sure they will provide the dog with a loving and suitable home.

Provide a written contract that clearly outlines the specific conditions of sale.

PART V

APPENDIX A

DOG GROUPS RECOGNIZED BY THE AMERICAN KENNEL CLUB

GROUP I: SPORTING DOGS
Brittany
Pointer
Pointer, German Shorthaired
Pointer, German Wirehaired
Retriever, Chesapeake Bay
Retriever, Curly-Coated
Retriever, Flat-Coated
Retriever, Golden
Retriever, Labrador
Setter, English
Setter, Gordon
Setter, Irish
Spaniel, American Water
Spaniel, Clumber
Spaniel, Cocker
Spaniel, English Cocker
Spaniel, English Springer
Spaniel, Field
Spaniel, Irish Water
Spaniel, Sussex
Spaniel, Welsh Springer
Vizsla
Weimaraner
Wirehaired Pointing Griffon

GROUP II: HOUNDS
Afghan Hound
Basenji
Basset Hound
Beagle
Black and Tan Coonhound
Bloodhound
Borzoi
Dachshund
Foxhound, American
Foxhound, English
Greyhound
Harrier
Ibizan Hound
Irish Wolfhound
Norwegian Elkhound
Otter Hound
Petits Bassets Griffon Vendeens
Pharaoh Hound
Rhodesian Ridgeback
Saluki
Scottish Deerhound
Whippet

GROUP III: WORKING DOGS
Akita
Alaskan Malamute
Bernese Mountain Dog
Boxer
Bullmastiff
Doberman Pinscher
Giant Schnauzer
Great Dane
Great Pyrenees
Komondor
Kuvasz
Mastiff
Newfoundland
Portuguese Water Dog
Rottweiler
St. Bernard
Samoyed
Siberian Husky
Standard Schnauzer

GROUP IV: TERRIERS
Airedale Terrier
American Staffordshire Terrier
Australian Terrier
Bedlington Terrier
Border Terrier
Bull Terrier
Cairn Terrier
Dandie Dinmont Terrier
Fox Terriers
Smooth Fox Terrier
Wire Fox Terrier
Irish Terrier
Kerry Blue Terrier
Lakeland Terrier
Manchester Terrier (Standard)
Miniature Schnauzer
Norfolk Terrier
Norwich Terrier
Scottish Terrier
Sealyham Terrier
Skye Terrier
Soft-Coated Wheaten Terrier
Staffordshire Bull Terrier
Welsh Terrier
West Highland White Terrier

GROUP V: TOYS

Affenpinscher
Brussels Griffon
Chihuahua
Chinese Crested
English Toy Spaniel
Italian Greyhound
Japanese Chin
Maltese
Manchester Terrier (Toy)
Miniature Pinscher
Papillon
Pekingese
Pomeranian
Poodle (Toy)
Pug
Shih Tzu
Silky Terrier
Yorkshire Terrier

GROUP VI: NON-SPORTING DOGS

Bichon Frise
Boston Terrier
Bulldog
Chow Chow
Dalmatian
Finnish Spitz
French Bulldog
Keeshond
Lhasa Apso
Poodle (Miniature and Standard)
Schipperke
Tibetan Spaniel
Tibetan Terrier

GROUP VII: HERDING DOGS

Australian Cattle Dog
Bearded Collie
Belgian Malinois
Belgian Sheepdog
Belgian Tervuren
Bouvier des Flandres
Briard
Collie
German Shepherd Dog
Old English Sheepdog
Puli
Shetland Sheepdog
Welsh Corgi, Cardigan
Welsh Corgi, Pembroke

APPENDIX B

BREED VARIETIES

Cocker Spaniels	Black (including Black and Tan), ASCOB, Parti-color
Beagles	13" and under, over 13" but not exceeding 15"
Dachshunds	Longhaired, Wirehaired, Smooth
Collies	Rough, Smooth
Bull Terriers	White, Colored
Manchester Terriers	Standard, Toy
Chihuahuas	Smooth Coat, Long Coat
English Toy Spaniels	King Charles and Ruby, Blenheim and Prince Charles
Poodles	Toy, Miniature, Standard

BREEDS IN WHICH COLOR MAY BE
A CONDITION OF A DIVISION OF A CLASS

Basenjis	Red, Black, Black and Tan
Boxers	Brindle, Fawn
Chow Chows	Black, Red, Any Other Color
Collies	Sable and White, Tri-Color, Blue Merle, White
Dachshunds	Open Class (Miniature) under 10 lbs. and 12 months of age and over. Open Class (Standard) 10 lbs. and over AND under 10 lbs. if less than 12 months of age. This class may also be divided by Red, Black and Tan. Any Other Color (Only the Dachshund Club of America may divide the Open Miniature Class by the above colors)
Dalmatians	Black Spotted, Liver Spotted
Doberman Pinschers	Black Any Other Allowed Color
English Cocker	Solid Color, to include any solid color, Spaniels except white, with Tan points Parti-color, including Roans and Ticks

Giant Schnauzers	Black, Pepper and Salt
Great Danes	Brindle, Fawn, Blue, Black, Harlequin
Labrador Retrievers	Black, Yellow, Chocolate
Newfoundlands	Black Other Than Black
Pekingese	Fawn, Bisquit, Grey, Red, Sable Parti-Color, Black Any Other Allowed Color
Pomeranian	Red, Orange, Cream and Sable Black, Brown and Blue Any Other Allowed Color
Pugs	Black, Fawn
Miniature Schnauzers	Salt and Pepper Black and Silver, Black
Shetland Sheepdogs	Sable, Sable and White, Blue Merle, Any Other Allowed Color
Japanese Chin	Black and White Red and White

BREEDS AND VARIETIES IN WHICH WEIGHT MAY BE A CONDITION OF DIVISION OF CLASS

Boston Terriers	Open classes: under 15 lbs, 15 lbs. and under 20 lbs., 20 lbs. and over (Also, under 15 lbs. and 15 lbs. and over)
Dachshunds	Open class (Miniature): under 10 lbs. and 12 months of age and over Open class (Standard): 10 lbs. and over and under 10 lbs. if less than 12 months of age
French Bulldogs	Open classes: under 22 lbs., and 22 lbs. and not over 28 lbs.
Italian Greyhounds	Open classes: 8 lbs. and under, over 8 lbs.
Japanese Chin	Open classes: 7 lbs. and under, over 7 lbs.
Manchester Terriers (Standard)	Open classes: over 12 lbs., not exceeding 16 lbs., over 16 lbs., not exceeding 22 lbs.
Manchester Terriers (Toy)	Open classes: 7 lbs. and under, over 7 lbs. and not exceeding 12 lbs. (Weight is a variety condition and becomes part of the conditions of every class)

| Pekingese
At All-Breed Shows | Open classes: under 8 lbs., if 12 months old or over, open, dogs, 8 lbs. or over (and under 8 lbs. if less than 12 months old) |
| At Specialty Show (or All-Breed if warranted by previous year's entry) | Open classes: under 6 lbs., if 12 months old or over, open, dogs, 6 lbs. and under 8 lbs., if 12 months old or over, open, dogs, 8 lbs. and over (and under 8 lbs if less than 12 months) |

BREEDS WHICH MAY HAVE CLASSES DIVIDED BASED ON BREED CHARACTERISTICS OTHER THAN WEIGHT, HEIGHT OR COLOR

Brussels Griffons	Rough coat, Smooth coat
Papillons	Erect ear, Drop ear
St. Bernards	Longhaired, Shorthaired
Salukis	Smooth Coat, Feather Coat
Skye Terriers	Drop Ears, Prick Ears

APPENDIX C

COLLECTION AND STORAGE FACILITIES FOR FROZEN CANINE SEMEN

The list below includes names of collection and storage facilities whose record-keeping practices have been examined and found to be in compliance with American Kennel Club regulations applying to the registration of litters produced artificially, using frozen semen. The AKC does not license, sponsor or endorse these facilities.

ARIZONA

Arizona Canine Semen Bank-Arizona
2611 West Northern Avenue
Phoenix AZ 85051
602/995-0460

CALIFORNIA

Canine Cryobank
330 North Andreasen Drive
Escondido CA 92025
619/739-1091

International Canine Genetics
3854 Santa Rosa Avenue
Santa Rosa CA 95407
707/573-1893

Spermco, Inc.
490 W. Durham Ferry Road
Tracy CA 95376
209/835-3259

GEORGIA

University of Georgia College
of Veterinary Medicine
Athens GA 30602
404/543-9368; 404/542-3221

ILLINOIS

Herd's Merchant Semen
7N330 Dunham Road
Elgin IL 60120
312/741-1444

International Canine Semen
Bank-Illinois
Route 78 North
Virginia IL 62691
217/452-3006; 217/323-2978

Seager Canine Semen Bank, Inc.
329 Sioux
Park Forest IL 60466
312/748-0954

Triple S. Cryo Genetics
University of Illinois Trail
Box 217
Philo IL 61864
217/684-2900; 217/253-3202

KENTUCKY

Premier Veterinary Services
Box 607
Shelbyville KY 40065
502/633-2000

MASSACHUSETTS

Westford-Ho Cryoservices
Elizabeth F. Trainor, VMD
Lovett Road
Oxford MA 01540
617/987-2110

MINNESOTA

Crossroads Animal Hospital, Ltd.
Frances O. Smith DVM, PhD
14321 Nicolett Court
Burnsville MN 55337
612/435-2655

OHIO

International Canine Semen
Bank-Ohio
34910 Center Ridge Road
North Ridgeville OH 44039
216/327-8282

OREGON

International Canine Semen
Bank-Oregon
Northwest Center
PO Box 651
Sandy OR 97055
503/663-7031; 503/663-1257

PENNSYLVANIA

Cryo-Genetic Laboratories
Ludwig's Corner, Route 100
and Blackhorse Road
Box 256-A
Chester Springs PA 19425
215/458-5888

International Canine Genetics
271 Great Valley Parkway
Malvern PA 19355
215/640-1244; 1/800/248-8099

SOUTH CAROLINA

Cryo Tech International, Inc.
Route 1, Box 386
Abbeville SC 29620
803/446-8787

TENNESSEE

Spring Creek Ranch and
Reproductive Center
Spring Creek Cyrogenics Division
380 S. Collierville-Arlington Road
Collierville TN 38017
901/853-0550

University of Tennessee
College of Veterinary Medicine
PO Box 1071
Knoxville TN 37901
617/546-9240

TEXAS

International Canine Semen
Bank-Texas
1236 Brittmoore
Houston TX 77073
713/468-8253

United Breeders Service
PO Box 211
Lubbock TX 79408
806/745-3419

VIRGINIA

Roanoke A. I. Laboratories, Inc.
8533 Martin Creek Road
Roanoke VA 24018
703/774-0676

WASHINGTON

Preservation, Inc.
17706 49th Place, S.E.
Snohomish WA 98290
206/568-8894

APPENDIX D

Completing An Entry Form

The owner of a dog has complete responsibility for ensuring that an entry form is complete and that the information given is accurate. Failure to give all of the necessary information could result in a rejection of the entry, and incorrect information could result in the entry being deemed invalid. The instructions and explanations given below should help to eliminate some of the common errors made in completing entry forms.

It would be acceptable to submit a photocopy of the entry form, but only if both sides of the form are attached together. This is necessary to ensure that the entrant has seen the agreement on the reverse side of the form. In signing the form, the owner or owner's agent are acknowledging that he or she is familiar with the *Rules Applying to Registrations and Dog Shows*, and the *Obedience Regulations*, if applicable. Single copies of these publications are available without charge from the American Kennel Club.

A sample entry form has been reproduced, with a letter designation given for each space. The instructions for completing each space follows, along with a list of breed varieties and allowable breed class divisions.

A) The name of the event-giving club and the date of the event must appear here. If a form for another event is being used, the printed information should be crossed out and the correct information added.

B) If the fee is not listed in the *GAZETTE*, it was not supplied by the club, and the Superintendent or Show Secretary listed for that event should be contacted.

C) See Chapter 6, Section 1, of the Dog Show Rules for the list of registrable breeds.

D) Breeds with Show Varieties are listed in Section 1.

E) The sex of the entry must appear here.

F) The regular dog show classes, along with the eligibility requirements for each, are listed in Chapter 6 of the Dog Show Rules.

G) The Puppy Classes may be divided into a 6 month and under 9 month class (6-9), and a 9 month and under 12 month class (9-12). THE CLASS DIVISION SHOULD *ALWAYS* BE INCLUDED TO ENSURE THAT THE ENTRY WILL BE ACCEPTED. IF A CLASS IS DIVIDED, AND NO DIVISION IS INDICATED ON THE ENTRY FORM, IT COULD BE REJECTED AS INCOMPLETE. Certain breeds do occasionally divide classes by color, weight or breed characteristics. The maximum allowable

OFFICIAL AMERICAN KENNEL CLUB ENTRY FORM

A)

I ENCLOSE $ **B)** for entry fees

IMPORTANT—Read Carefully Instructions on Reverse Side Before Filling Out. Numbers in the boxes indicate sections of the instructions relevant to the information needed in that box (PLEASE PRINT)

BREED **C)**	VARIETY [1] **D)**	SEX **E)**

DOG [2] [3] SHOW CLASS **F)**	CLASS [ ] DIVISION Weight color etc **G)**

ADDITIONAL CLASSES	OBEDIENCE TRIAL CLASS	JR SHOWMANSHIP CLASS

NAME OF (See Back) JUNIOR HANDLER (if any)

FULL NAME OF DOG

Enter number here

AKC REG NO AKC LITTER NO ILP NO	DATE OF BIRTH
FOREIGN REG NO & COUNTRY	PLACE OF [ ] USA [ ] Canada [ ] Foreign BIRTH Do not print the above in catalog

BREEDER

SIRE

DAM

ACTUAL OWNER(S) _____
[4]   (Please Print)

OWNER'S ADDRESS _____

CITY _____ STATE _____ ZIP _____

NAME OF OWNERS AGENT
(IF ANY) AT THE SHOW _____

I CERTIFY that I am the actual owner of the dog, or that I am the duly authorized agent of the actual owner whose name I have entered above. In consideration of the acceptance of this entry, I (we) agree to abide by the rules and regulations of The American Kennel Club in effect at the time of this show or obedience trial, and by any additional rules and regulations appearing in the premium list for this show or obedience trial or both, and further agree to be bound by the "Agreement" printed on the reverse side of this entry form. I (we) certify and represent that the dog entered is not a hazard to persons or other dogs. This entry is submitted for acceptance on the foregoing representation and agreement.

SIGNATURE of owner or his agent
duly authorized to make this entry _____

TELEPHONE # _____

---

divisions in each breed are listed in Sections 2, 3 and 4. IT IS RECOMMENDED THAT THE APPROPRIATE COLOR, WEIGHT OR BREED CHARACTERISTIC *ALWAYS* BE INCLUDED ON AN ENTRY FORM, JUST IN CASE A PARTICULAR SHOW DOES DIVIDE THE BREED CLASSES.

H) If a dog is entered in more than one class, the additional classes should be included here.

I) This space is for the first obedience class entered.

J) This space is for any Junior Showmanship class entered. The space on the reverse side of the form must also be completed.

K) The name of the Junior Handler, if applicable, must appear here.

L) The full name of the dog, with correct spelling, must appear here.

M) The correct registration number must be given, and the applicable box checked. If the number used is foreign, the country of birth must be given. See Chapter 14, Section 1, of the Dog Show Rules for information on the entry of dogs under an AKC litter or foreign registration number.

N) The date of birth must be given for an entry in the Puppy or Twelve-to-Eighteen month class.

O) The place of birth must be checked for an entry in every regular class but Open or Best of Breed.

P) The name of the breeder must be given for an entry in the Bred-by-Exhibitor class.

Q)
and
R) This information is optional but must be correct and complete if given.

S) The name of the actual owner must be given (see Chapter 14, Section 3, of the Dog Show Rules).

T) If it is known that someone other than the owner will have charge of the dog at the show, the name of that other person should appear here.

U) If someone other than the owner has been authorized by the owner to make the entry, that person must sign the entry form.

V) If there is a problem with the entry that is picked up prior to closing, many Superintendents or Show and Trial Secretaries will try to contact the exhibitor as a courtesy, even though not required to do so under the Rules.

W) This information must be supplied if the entry is for Junior Showmanship.

ENCLOSE $ _____ for entry fees

IMPORTANT—Read Carefully Instructions on Reverse instructions relevant to the information needed in that

BREED

DOG [2] [3] SHOW CLASS _____ Weight color etc

ADDITIONAL CLASSES **H)** | OBEDIENCE TRIAL CLASS **I)** | JR SHOWMANSHIP CLASS **J)**

NAME OF (See Back) JUNIOR HANDLER (if any) **K)**

FULL NAME OF DOG **L)**

Enter number here

☐ AKC REG NO
☐ AKC LITTER NO
☐ ILP NO
☐ FOREIGN REG NO & COUNTRY **M)** | DATE OF BIRTH **N)** | PLACE OF ☐ USA ☐ Canada ☐ Foreign BIRTH **O)** Do not print the above in catalog

BREEDER **P)**

SIRE **Q)**

DAM **R)**

ACTUAL OWNER(S) _____ **S)**
[4] (Please Print)
OWNER'S ADDRESS _____
CITY _____ STATE _____ ZIP _____

NAME OF OWNERS AGENT **T)**
(IF ANY) AT THE SHOW _____

I CERTIFY that I am the actual owner of the dog, or that I am the duly authorized agent of the actual owner whose name I have entered above. In consideration of the acceptance of this entry, I (we) agree to abide by the rules and regulations of The American Kennel Club in effect at the time of this show or obedience trial, and by any additional rules and regulations appearing in the premium list for this show or obedience trial or both, and further agree to be bound by the "Agreement" printed on the reverse side of this entry form. I (we) certify and represent that the dog entered is not a hazard to persons or other dogs. This entry is submitted for acceptance on the foregoing representation and agreement.

SIGNATURE of owner or his agent duly authorized to make this entry _____ **U)**
TELEPHONE # _____ **V)**

entering your dog is divided, then, in class in which you are entering your dog

4 A dog must be entered in the name a registered dog has been acqui show for which entries closed a received the registration certificate whether transfer application has been mailed to A.K.C. complete the following

If this entry is for Jr Showmanship please give the following information

JR'S DATE OF BIRTH _____

JUNIOR SHOWMANSHIP
ADDRESS _____ **W)**
CITY _____ STATE _____ ZIP _____

If Jr Handler is not the owner of the dog identified on the face of this form, what is the relationship of the Jr Handler to the owner?

APPENDIX E

EXAMPLES OF RECORD FORMS

Show Record

Show	Date	Dog(s) Entered	Wins	Judge

Boarding Record

Dog's Name	Breed	Rate	Owner's Name Address & Phone	Date: In	To Go	Remarks*

*Remarks should contain feeding and other special instructions, grooming to be done, addresses of friends, etc. (Use two or more lines per dog if necessary).

Litter Record

Bitch _____ Sire _____ Bred To: _____

AKC No. _____

Dam _____ Dates: _____

Litter Reg. No. _____ Date Whelped: _____

Pup No.	1	2	3	4	5	6	7
Name							
Reg. No.							
Sex							
Color, Markings							
Disposed of							
Remarks							

Inventory of Dogs: _____ 19_____

AKC No.	Sex	Name	Date Whelped	Sire	Dam	Disposal	Value

Kennel Bitches Bred

Name	Date In	Date Bred	Stud	Date Wormed	Date Whelped	Puppies Alive	Puppies Dead

Outside Bitches Bred

Name	Owner's Name & Address	Date Rec'd.	Dates Bred	Stud Used	Remarks

Treatment Record

Date	Name	Remarks

This is a sample of the type of record card which provides space for complete information on an entire litter. "Type of Birth" would show whether puppies were born normally, by breech, etc. "Condition" would indicate whether a puppy appeared to be normal or was undershot, etc. Entries under "Notes" would show whether a puppy was sold, given away, etc. To be more complete, photographs should be kept of each puppy, with the dates. Further, a record of the show career should be attached for each wining offspring.

LITTER RECORD

Date of Birth:
Type of Birth:
Sire: Dam:
Number of Puppies: Alive: Stillborn:
Pedigree

Number	Sex	Color	Condition	Notes

This is a sample of the type of record card that should be maintained for each individual dog and bitch owned by a breeder.

INDIVIDUAL PROGENY RECORD

Dog: Sex:
Dam: Sire:
Date of Birth:
AKC Registration Number:
Color:
Quality Score:
Temperament Score:
Health Record:
Date of Death: Cause of Death:
Health Score: Age at Death:
Number in Litter at Birth:
Number Surviving to 8 Weeks: M: F:

This shows the type of information to be entered on the back of the "Individual Progeny Record" card to provide a complete breeding record for a female.

BREEDING RECORD – FEMALE

Dates of Heats	Dates Mated	Dog	Date Whelped	Litter Number

This shows the type of information to be entered on the back of the "Individual Progeny Record" card to provide a complete breeding record for a male.

BREEDING RECORD – MALE

Dates Mated	Bitch	Litter Number	Number of Puppies	Sex M F

Glossary

Afghan Hound	Descended from the Persian Greyhounds of antiquity. Hunts by sight. A member of the Hound Group.
Afterbirth	The placenta attached to the sac in which puppy is born.
American Kennel Club (AKC)	The governing and registration body along with the United Kennel Club for purebred dogs.
AKC Field Representative	AKC's official representative on site at dog shows. Interprets and monitors adherence to rules. Evaluates judges, administers judge's tests and answers exhibitor's questions.
AKC Gazette	A monthly publication of the AKC containing articles, statistics about shows and registrations and official and proposed actions of the AKC.
All-Breed Club	A club devoted to the showing and breeding of purebred dogs. Membership is open to breeders and exhibitors of all breeds. Holds championship shows.
All-Breed Show	An AKC-approved show in which all AKC-approved breeds can be exhibited.
American Water Spaniel	Ancestry is clouded but suggests Irish Water Spaniel and Curly Coated Retriever. A good little hunter. A member of the Sporting Group.
Arbiters	Dog-show judges.
Artificial Insemination	Impregnating a bitch with frozen or extended sperm.
Awkward Phase	Rapid-growth period for a puppy usually associated with plaining out of the head features. Occurs from three to eight months.
Back	That portion of the topline starting just behind the withers and ending where the croup and loin join.

Backcrossing	To cross a first generation hybrid with one of the parents.
Baiting	Keeping a dog alert in the ring through the use of food or a favorite toy.
Balance	Overall fitting of the various parts of the dog to give a picture of symmetry and correct interaction.
Basenji	An African barkless dog. A member of the Hound Group.
Best Of Breed	Best of that breed in an all-breed or specialty show. In the all-breed show it goes on to compete for higher awards.
Best In Show	Top award in an all-breed show.
Best Of Variety	Top award for breeds that are divided by variety based on coat, color or size.
Best Of Winners	Defeats other sex winner. Captures that sex's points if greater than its own on that day.
Bitch	A female dog.
Bite	Position of upper and lower teeth in relation to each other. Various breed standards call for different kinds of bite often based on function.
Bloodline	A specific strain or type within a breed.
Bottle Feeding	Using a doll bottle to feed formula to a newborn puppy.
Breaking Point	Limit to what the dog can endure.
Breech Presentation	Puppy born feet first rather than head first. Can cause whelping difficulties as puppy may get turned sideways in the birth canal.
Breed Ring	Exhibition area where dogs are judged by breed.

Brittany	A leggy, close-coupled dog who is an excellent combination hunter, pointer and retriever. A member of the Sporting Group.
Brucellosis	A sexually transmitted disease or infection.
Brussels Griffon	Many small dogs went into the creation of this breed. His popularity grows. A member of the Toy Group.
Bulbus Glandis	A portion of the penis closest to the testicles which fills with blood to three times its size during the sexual act. It serves to "tie" the male and female together while the male ejaculates sperm.
Caesarean Section	Removing puppies from the womb surgically.
Cairn Terrier	Feisty little terrier with a great love of people. His breeding is handed down from the old working terriers on the British Isle of Skye. A member of the Terrier Group.
Campaigning A Dog	Seriously exhibiting a champion to compete for top honors in his breed, group and top 10 all- breed honors.
Canine Herpes Virus	An infection in puppies caused by an infected dam. A leading cause of puppy mortality.
Canine Parvovirus	Myocardial forms attack only puppies. Severe, often fatal reaction. Cardial form attacks older dogs.
Caveat emptor	Latin for "let the buyer beware."
Championship	A title earned by winning 15 points under AKC rules, including two major awards of 3, 4 or 5 points under two different judges.
Championship Points	Awarded on the basis of the number of dogs competing by sex and breed. Each part of the country has a different point rating based upon previous year's entries. Maximum number of points per show is 5. Fifteen are needed for a championship, with two major awards among them.

Cheetah	The fastest land animal for short distances.
Chromosome	Cell nucleus of all multicell organisms that contain DNA. Comprising the genes of that species.
Collie	A medium-sized dog (rough-coated and smooth-coated varieties) that was developed to herd sheep. A member of the Herding Group.
Colostrum	A part of the bitch's milk which provides puppies immunity from many viral and bacterial diseases.
Cocker Spaniel	Smallest member of the Sporting Group. Bred to flush and retrieve upland game.
Contour	Silhouette or profile, form or shape.
Conformation	The form and structure of the various parts to fit a standard.
Corgi (Welsh)	Two varieties are Cardigan and Pembroke. A small, hardy dog used to herd cattle. A member of the Herding Group.
Crabbing	Moving with body at an angle with the line of travel like a land crab. Also called sidewinding.
Crapshoot Theory	Senior author's definition of anything can happen at any time in purebred dogs.
Crate	A metal, plastic or wood kennel (in various sizes). Dogs may sleep and travel in them.
Cropped	Trimming the ears to fit a breed pattern.
Cryptorchid	A male dog with neither testicle descended. Ineligible to compete at AKC shows.
Dachshund	A small, longish dog bred to go to ground after game. A member of the Hound Group.
Dalmatian	The black and white spotted dog. A member of the Non-Sporting Group.

Dam	Mother of a litter of puppies.
Degeneration	Used in reference to inbreeding. After primary generations, stock shows reduction in size, bone and vigor.
Dehydration	Loss of body fluids - may lead to death.
Developmental Phases	Stages through which puppies grow.
Dew Claws	Hardy nails above pastern. Most breeds have them removed. In many breeds they are not present.
DNA	Deoxyribonucleic acid - genes are made up of DNA. They are regarded as the building blocks of life.
Dominant	Color or characteristic that covers up all others which are recessive to it.
Docking	The clipping off of the tail to a prescribed length to meet a breed standard.
Doberman	A working dog originally bred in Germany. A quick and strong animal. A member of the Working Group.
Dropper-feeding	Feeding formula to newborn puppies through the use of a small medicine dropper.
Eclampsia	An attack of convulsions during and after pregnancy.
Egg	A female reproductive cell.
Estrus	Period of bitch's heat cycle when she is ready to breed.
Exhibitors	People who show their dogs.
Expression	Facial aspect or countenance.
Eye For A Dog	An old dog game expression meaning the ability to select a good dog without a lot of effort.

Fading Puppy Syndrome	A malnourished puppy due to loss of electrolytes. May lead to death.
Fallopian Tubes	Conduits for eggs from ovary to uterus.
Fetus	The growing puppy within the womb.
Filial Regression	The tendency of offspring to regress toward mediocrity if controlled breeding is not carried out.
Finishable	A dog capable of completing its championship.
Fluid Pressure	Pressure caused by pumping action of the heart as the blood flows through the veins and arteries.
Forechest	The point of the thorax that protrudes beyond the point of the shoulder.
Foreface	That part of the muzzle from just below the forehead to the nose.
First Call Dog	Handler selects one of his dogs to show at group level if he has more than one breed winner in that group. Same applies to handler who wins two or more groups when selecting dog for Best In Show. Usually selected by client or dog's seniority or additional money paid for that honor.
Gaiting	Walking or trotting a dog to discern proper movement.
Gene	The smallest unit of hereditary information.
Genetics	The study of the science of heredity.
Genotype	Genetic term meaning the unseen genetic makeup of the dog.
Gestation	The organic development of the puppy within the uterus.
German Shepherd	A versatile working dog. Originally bred in Germany to guard and herd. A member of the Herding Group.

German Shorthaired Pointer	A continental gun dog. Bred for game. A member of the Sporting Group.
German Wirehaired Pointer	A Hunter-Pointer-Retriever breed with a harsh, wiry coat. A member of the Sporting Group.
Golden Retriever	A mid-size, heavy-coated dog used for both water and upland game. A member of the Sporting Group.
Gordon Setter	A black and tan hunting dog. Heavier than the English and Irish Setters. A member of the Sporting Group.
Gravity	The pull of the earth upon a body.
Great Dane	A very large dog whose history shows it to have been used to hunt wild boar and as a war dog. A member of the Working Group.
Greyhound	The oldest pure breed in existence. He hunts by sight. A member of the Hound Group.
Groom	To comb, clip and brush a dog.
Grooming Table	A specially designed (often foldable) table with matting for grooming and training dogs.
Handler	Person showing the dog.
Handler's Apprentice	A person learning the handler's trade.
Handler's Assistant	Usually a person who has graduated to the next rung on the career ladder.
Handlers Guild	An association of professional handlers stressing professionalism.
Heat	A bitch coming into season so she can be bred. Usually twice a year.
Heredity	The sum of what a dog inherits from preceding generations.
Hetrozygous	Non-dominant for a trait or color. Carries both dominant and recessive genes for a variety of traits.

Homozygous	Dominant for a trait or color. Carries no recessive for that characteristic.
Hybrid	Dogs who have gene pairs -- non-dominant.
Hybrid Vigor	The extra vigor or development exhibited by offspring of an outcross.
Hyperthermia	A chilling of the puppies which is liable to cause death.
Idling Speed	Energy consumed when body is not in kinetic motion.
Inbreeding	Very close familial breeding, i.e., brother X sister, father X daughter or son X mother.
Inguinal Ring	Muscles of the abdominal cavity (groin) that prevent adult testes from going back up into abdominal cavity and, which can prevent their proper descent in puppies.
Irish Setter	A tall, mahogany-red dog of striking style. A hunting dog of the Sporting Group.
Irish Water Spaniel	An exuberant, red, curly-coated hunting dog with a monkey-like tail. An excellent hunter and a member of the Sporting Group.
Irish Wolfhound	This is a massive dog. Bred to chase and kill wolves he is now a gentle pet. A member of the Hound Group.
Judge	A person approved by AKC or UKC to judge various breeds.
Kinetic Energy	Relating to the motion of bodies and the forces and energy associated therewith.
Komondor	An Hungarian sheep and cattle dog. Excellent as a guardian of the flock or herd. A member of the Working Group.
Labor	The act of attempting to whelp puppies.
Labrador Retriever	A wonderful water retriever. His Otter tail is unique. A member of the Sporting Group.

Lakeland Terrier	A dog of English origin bred to kill fox that hound pack had run to ground in rocky den. A member of the Terrier Group.
Lead	A strap or cord fastened around dog's neck to guide him. Also called leash.
Lead Training	Teaching the dog to walk and trot properly so as to best exhibit his conformation. May also be used for control.
Levers	Angles to improve multiplication of force.
Line Breeding	Breeding closely within a family of dogs, i.e., grandfather to granddaughter.
Match Show	A practice show that serves as a training ground for young dogs, prospective judges and members of the dog club holding the show.
Malnutrition	Lacking the proper nourishment to provide normal healthy growth.
Gregor Mendel	A monk in 19th Century Czechoslovakia who discovered the mathematical formulas for the inheritance of color and size in sweet peas and launched the science of genetics.
Metritis	A uterine infection in the dam that can transmit bacterial infection to an entire litter.
Monorchid	A male dog with only one testicle descended. Ineligible to compete in AKC shows.
Monstrosities	Severe, often lethal deviations from expected structure, usually brought out through inbreeding.
Nasal Aspirator	A suction device for sucking mucous from infant puppies' nasal passages.
Natural Selection	Charles Darwin's theory of how species evolve.
Neonatal	New born.

Neonatal Septecemia	An infection in newborn puppies picked up by staphylococcus germs in the dam's vaginal tract.
Non-Dominant	An animal with characteristics that are mostly recessive.
Nucleus	The center of a cell. Contains chromosomes and is essential to all cell functions, such as cell division for reproduction.
Otter Hound	A Standard-Poodle-sized dog originally bred in England to hunt otters. A member of the Hound Group.
Outcrossing	Matings of animals that are somewhat inbred to unrelated animals to reinstate vigor and substance.
Ovulation	The female process of creating eggs for reproduction.
Ovum	An egg ready for sperm to fertilize it.
Parasites	Infestations of lice, ticks or fleas as well as internal infestation of various worms.
Pastern	The body's shock absorber. Located at the juncture where the paw meets foreleg.
Pedigree	Hierarchical listing of ancestors. Best used when combined with photos and anecdotal data.
PHA	Professional Handlers Association. A group stressing ethics and training.
Pharaoh Hound	One of the oldest domesticated dogs in written history. Images of this type of dog are found on ancient Egyptian paintings. A member of the Hound Group.
Phenotype	The actual outward appearance as can be seen--opposite of genotype.
Placenta	A vascular organ that links the fetus to the dam's uterus. Nourishes and mediates fetal change. Also known as an afterbirth.

Plaining Out	Usually occurs as head changes because of the loss of puppy teeth.
Pointer	A breed of dog used for pointing birds. The modern dog comes from England by way of Spain. A member of the Sporting Group.
Poodle	This popular breed comes in three sizes, Standard, Miniature and Toy. The Standard and Miniature are to be found in the Non-Sporting Group with their diminutive cousin in the Toy Group.
Portuguese Water Dog	An ancient working dog who was bred to help herd fish into nets and act as a courier between ships. A member of the Working Group.
Postpartum	After birth.
Pounding	Results when front stride is shorter than rear. Hindquarter thrust forces front feet to strike the ground before they are fully prepared to absorb shock.
Pregnant	Term used for bitch carrying puppies.
Producing Power	The ability to stamp one's get with positive features of championship caliber.
Proestrus	First part of heat cycle.
Professional Handler	A person paid to show and train dogs.
Profile	Outline or silhouette.
Proportion	Relationship, ratio of one body part to another.
Proven Sire	Male dog that has enough offspring to judge his potency.
Puli	An Hungarian shepherd dog. His name means driver. A member of the Herding Group.
Puppy Septicemia	Bacterial infection caused by a mastitis infection in the dam. Often fatal if not treated immediately.

Purebred	A dog whose sire and dam are of the same breed and whose lineage is unmixed with any other breed.
Quarantine	A period in which a dog is isolated from other animals while being observed for communicable diseases.
Recessive	Color or trait which is not dominant and must link up with another recessive for expression.
Reserve Winners	Dog or bitch that is runner up to the winner. May gain points if winner is ineligible or is disqualified.
Ribs	The thorasic vertebrae that surround the heart and lungs.
Rin Tin Tin	A German Shepherd Dog who was a star in the early days of the film industry.
Ringside Pickup	When a handler takes on a dog on the day of the show rather than having him in his traveling string of dogs.
Ring Stewards	Persons assisting the judge by assembling classes, giving out armbands, arranging ribbons, and in general, being an assistant for the judge.
Russian Wolfhound	Officially known as the Borzoi. Hunts by sight. A member of the Hound Group.
Sac	Membrane housing puppy within uterus.
Saluki	A tall, sleek dog that hunts by sight. A member of the Hound Group.
Scrotum	Housing for male dogs testicles.
Sheltie	Known as the Shetland Sheepdog. A working Collie in miniature. A member of the Herding Group.
Show Pose	Setting a dog in a position to exhibit its conformation. Also called stacking.

Showmanship	The bravura exhibition of a dog.
Show Superintendent	A person (organization) hired by club giving show to manage and run the show.
Sidewinding	See Crabbing.
Sire	Father of a litter.
Special	A champion dog or bitch competing for Best of Breed or Best of Variety award. A class for champions only.
Specialty Club	A club devoted to fanciers of one specific breed of dog.
Specialty Show	An AKC-approved show for members of a single breed only.
Spermatozoa	Motile sperm from male dog.
Spoon-Feeding	Slowly feeding milk formula to baby puppy using a small spoon.
Springer (Spaniel)	Two different breeds included in this appellation. English Springer and Welsh Springer. Both members of the Sporting Group.
Stacking	See Show Pose.
Standard	An official description of the breed developed by that breed's parent club and approved by AKC.
Structural Design	The blueprint from which the originators of a breed sought to create a dog for the task at hand.
Subcutaneous Muscle	That type of muscle which lies directly under the skin.
Symmetry	A pleasing balance of all parts.
Test Breeding	A mating usually of a parent of unknown genotype and one of a known genotype to reveal what characteristics the unknown one will throw.

Tie	The locking together of the dog and bitch during mating caused by the swelling of the Bulbis Glandis just behind the penis bone.
Topline	That portion of the dog's outline from the withers to the set on of the tail.
Toxic Milk Syndrome	Toxic bacteria in dam's milk having a toxic effect on nursing puppies.
Tube-Feeding	Inserting a tube down the esophagus into the puppy's stomach to release milk formula slowly.
Type	Characteristics distinguishing a breed.
Unbroken Line	A pedigree line of continuous producers down to the current sire or dam.
Umbilical cord	A cord that connects the fetus with the placenta attaching at the puppy's navel.
Vaccinations	Shots administered to ward off certain diseases.
Vals Theory	A classification of people (group) types developed by the Stanford Research Institute.
Vizsla	A continental gun dog from Hungary bred for hunting, pointing and retrieving. A member of the Sporting Group.
Vulva	External parts (lips) of bitch's genital organs.
Wean	Gradually changing puppies to solid food away from mother's milk.
Weimaraner	A grey hunting dog from Germany who points his game. A member of the Sporting Group.
Whelping Box	Where you wish to have the litter born and the bitch doesn't. Used later for nursing bitch and her puppies.
Winners (Dog & Bitch)	Best from all the competing classes. Wins points toward championship.

Withers	Highest point on the shoulder blades.
WYSIWYG	What you see is what you get. A desktop publishing term. Here applied to a dominant animal who throws the characteristics you see.

BIBLIOGRAPHY

BOOKS

Benn, Alec, *The 27 Most Common Mistakes in Advertising*. New York: American Management Association, 1978.

Bulanda, Susan, *The Canine Source Book*. Wilsonville, OR: Doral, 1990.

Coe, Susan, *The Basenji: Out of Africa to You*. Wilsonville, OR: Doral, 1990.

Connett, Eugene V., *American Sporting Dogs*. D. Van Nostrand Co., Inc.

Cornyn-Selby, Alice P., *Why Do Winners Win*. Beynch Press, 1989.

Craig, Ralph, *Elementary Spaniel Field Training*. New York: American Spaniel Club, 1947.

Daniels, Julie, *Enjoying Dog Agility from Backyard to Competition*. Wilsonville, OR: Doral, 1991.

Greer, Frances (Editor), *A Century of Spaniels;* Vols. I & II. Amherst, MA: American Spaniel Club, 1980.

Grossman, Dr. Alvin, *American Cocker Spaniel*. Wilsonville, OR: Doral, 1988.

Grossman, Dr. Alvin, *Breeding Better Cocker Spaniels*. Fairfax, VA: Denlinger, 1977.

Grossman, Dr. Alvin, *Great American Dog Show Game*. Fairfax, VA: Denlinger, 1985.

Grossman, Dr. Alvin, *The Standard Book of Dog Breeding: A New Look*. Wilsonville, OR: Doral, 1991.

Hutt, Frederick B., *Genetics for Dog Breeders*. San Francisco: Freeman & Co., 1979.

Jackson, Tony (Editor), *Hunter Pointer Retriever: The Continental Gundog*. England: Ashford Press, 1989.

Miller, Jonathan, *The Body in Question*. New York: Random House, 1978.

Moffit, Ella, B., *The Cocker Spaniel: Companion, Shooting Dog and Show Dog*. New York: Orange Judd Publishing Co., 1949.

Pfaffenberger, Clarence, *New Knowledge of Dog Behavior*. New York: Howell Book House, 1963.

Sabella, Frank and Kalstone, Shirlee, *The Art of Handling Dog Shows*. Hollywood: B & E Publications, 1980.

Smith, Anthony, *The Human Pedigree*. Philadelphia: J.B. Lippincott Co., 1975.

Tayton, Mark (revised and updated by Silk, Sheila T.), *Successful Kennel Management*, Fourth Edition. Taylors, SC: Beech Tree Publishing Co., 1984.

Whitney, Leon F., DVM, *This is the Cocker Spaniel*. New York: Orange Judd Publishing Co., 1947.

Wolters, Richard A., *Game Dog*. New York: E.P. Dutton & Co., 1983.

Wolters, Richard A., *Gun Dog*. New York: E.P. Dutton, 1961.

PERIODICALS

Anderson, Carolyn, *Brittany World*, Spring 1991.

Dunbar, Ian Dr., "Breeding the Best," *American Kennel Gazette*, May 1991.

Grossman, Dr. Alvin, "Color Inheritance," *The American Cocker Review*, March, April, May, June, 1974.

Grossman, Dr. Alvin, "Faults and Double Faults," *The American Cocker Review*, March 1980.

Grossman, Marge, "Evolution of the Cocker Head," *The American Cocker Review*, June 1961.

Grossman, Marge, "To the Victors," *The American Cocker Review*, August 1966

Vargo, Stephanie, "Limited Registration Update," *American Kennel Gazette*, May 1991.

NEWSPAPERS

Chicago Tribune
Portland *Oregonian*, July 1, 1991.

VIDEOS

A Day in the Ring with Mr. Wrong, American Kennel Club.
Puppies, Puppies: Here They Come, Ready or Not, Doral.

INDEX